OPEN WORLD

B1

PRELIMINARY

WORKBOOK WITH ANSWERS

with Audio Download

Sheila Dignen

with Sarah Dymond

Cambridge University Press
www.cambridge.org/elt

Cambridge Assessment English
www.cambridgeenglish.org

Information on this title: www.cambridge.org/9781108759243

© Cambridge University Press and UCLES 2019

First published 2019

20 19 18 17 16 15 14 13 12 11 10 9 8 7 6 5 4

Printed in Malaysia by Vivar Printing

A catalogue record for this publication is available from the British Library

ISBN 978-1-108-75924-3 Workbook with answers with Audio Download

CONTENTS

S PERSONAL PROFILE

VOCABULARY

1 Write the words for the personal interests.

1

m _____ c

2

t _____ _____ l

3

f _____ _____ n

4

c _____ g

5

s _____ s

6

a _____ s and
c _____ s

2 Complete the sentences with the correct form of the verbs in the box.

| buy   cook   learn   listen   make   play |

1 I like _____ to music.

2 My brother enjoys _____ football and other sports.

3 Elsie loves _____ new clothes – that's why she never has any money!

4 I enjoy _____ meals for my family.

5 My sister likes _____ things, so she does a lot of arts and crafts.

6 I love _____ about different fashions in the past.

3 Choose the correct words to complete the text.

During the week, I usually get ¹*up / out / in* quite early, then I ²*do / have / make* a shower and get dressed. I ³*do / go / have* breakfast at about 7.30, and then I pick up my bag and ⁴*leave / get / go* to college. I have classes all morning, then I ⁵*take / have / go* lunch with my friends before the afternoon classes. I don't usually meet ⁶*up / out / to* with my friends in the evenings, because I have a part-time job as a waiter. When I'm not working, I like keeping fit, so I often work ⁷*up / out / off* at the gym. At the weekends, I often hang ⁸*up / off / out* with my friends. We sometimes eat ⁹*up / out / over*, but not too often because it's quite expensive.

4 Read the clues that people give about their occupations. Write the occupations.

1 I enjoy helping customers choose the right things to buy.
I'm a s_____ a_____.

2 I love food and cooking, so this is my dream job!
I'm a c_____.

3 My job is important to help people know what's happening in the world.
I'm a j_____.

4 I love working outside, and it's great when I see my plants growing.
I'm a g_____.

5 Without me, there would be a lot more crime.
I'm a p_____ o_____.

6 You come to me if you have a problem with your car.
I'm a m_____.

7 I love chatting to people while I make their hair look amazing.
I'm a h_____.

GRAMMAR

1 Complete the sentences with the present simple or present continuous form of the verbs in brackets. Remember to think about the position of the adverbs of frequency.

1 My brother _____ (never / get up) early!

2 Mmm, I _____ (enjoy) this soup – it's lovely!

3 Bankers _____ (usually / earn) a lot of money.

4 My sister _____ (always / borrow) my clothes without asking. It's so annoying!

5 More people _____ (become) vegetarians now.

6 Hollywood films _____ (often / be) really exciting.

7 I _____ (not / read) a book at the moment. Can you recommend one?

8 Tim _____ (not like) cooking.

9 My dad _____ (always / tell) really bad jokes in front of my friends. It's so embarrassing!

10 Jack _____ (not work) as a gardener at the moment.

2 Complete the questions with the question words in the box and then match them to the answers a–f.

| how | what | when | where | who | why |

1. _____ do you live?
2. _____ do you hang out with at the weekend?
3. _____ are your exams?
4. _____ old are you?
5. _____ do you do on Saturdays?
6. _____ are you happy today?

a With my friends.
b Because it's the weekend!
c I often go shopping.
d I live in London.
e They're next month.
f I'm nineteen.

3 Write the words in the correct order to make questions.

1. you / doing / what / are

   _____?

2. what time / film / start / does / the

   _____?

3. who / Max / is / to / talking

   _____?

4. home / going / now / they / are

   _____?

5. Sam / restaurant / work / in / does / a

   _____?

6. what / usually / have / you / do / for breakfast

   _____?

4 Complete the posts with the correct verb forms.

What do you love and hate about Mondays?

JayT44
At the moment I ¹ _____ (study) to be a doctor. Mondays are difficult for me because I ² _____ (usually / be) tired after the weekend! Why ³ _____ (the weekends / go) so quickly?

EllieZZ
I ⁴ _____ (go / sometimes) away with friends for the weekend. It's great, except my friend Anna ⁵ _____ (always / borrow) my clothes and make-up – it's really annoying when I can't find something I need for work on Monday morning!

Joe99
I'm a student, and on Mondays I ⁶ _____ (have) a really difficult maths class. I have to study maths because I ⁷ _____ (train) to be a mechanic, but I ⁸ _____ (hate) it!

1 ◎ 02 Listen to three young people talking about their jobs and daily routines. Choose the job that each person does or wants to do.

1. Maria
   restaurant chef / cookery vlogger / food writer
2. Sam
   teacher / sports photographer / tennis player
3. Anika
   journalist / police officer / doctor

2 ◎ 02 Listen again and write M (Maria), S (Sam) or A (Anika).

Which person …?
1. doesn't want to work in the evenings _____
2. is working and also studying _____
3. doesn't often eat out _____
4. is interested in music _____
5. wants to travel in the future _____
6. meets different people as part of their job _____

3 ◎ 03 Complete the sentences with one word in each gap. Listen and check.

1. I'm really interested _____ food.
2. I don't want to work _____ a chef in a restaurant.
3. I'm winning quite a lot of games _____ the moment.
4. I also listen _____ music a lot at home.
5. I also work _____ a newspaper in my town.
6. This is the right job _____ me.

READING

1 Read an interview with Tom, a British man who is working as a ninja in Japan. Match questions a–g with gaps 1–6. There is one question you don't need.

a Is it difficult to become a ninja?
b What is a ninja?
c Is there anything you don't like about the job?
d What's your daily routine like?
e What special clothes do ninjas wear?
f What do you enjoy the most about your job?
g What does a professional ninja do nowadays?

(1) ....

Ninjas are traditional fighters in Japan. They usually fight using their hands. They also use high jumps and kicks, so they're very fit. There aren't any real ninjas now, but people still learn the skills because ninjas are important in Japanese culture.

(2) ....

Some towns and cities in Japan employ ninjas because tourists like them. The ninjas put on shows of their skills in the streets. They also talk to tourists about the ninja traditions. Tourists also love taking photos of themselves with a ninja!

(3) ....

Yes, it is. You have to be very fit, and you have to practise a lot to learn all the skills. You also need a good memory, because you need to learn about the history of ninjas and why they're important in Japanese culture.

(4) ....

I get up early and have a light breakfast. Then I practise my skills for two hours. I often practise with other ninjas, which is fun. Then at 10.30 I start work in the city centre. We do four or five shows a day, so it's quite tiring. Then in the evenings I usually work out for an hour, because you need to be strong to be a ninja. So there isn't much time for hanging out with friends!

(5) ....

Everything! I really like learning the ninja skills. You feel so good when you manage to do something new. At the moment I'm trying to learn a really difficult move, and I love that challenge. I also enjoy talking to the tourists, especially the kids. They're funny because they always want to fight me!

(6) ....

Yes, I hate the fact that I can't have chips or chocolate! Ninjas have to be small and not very heavy, so I'm very careful about what I eat. But it's worth it so I can do a job that I love.

2 Read the text again. Decide if the sentences are true or false.

1 There are still a few real ninjas in Japan.
2 Modern ninjas work to entertain tourists.
3 You have to learn skills and study to become a ninja.
4 Tom spends a lot of time relaxing with friends.
5 Tom finds children annoying when he's working.
6 Tom can't eat all the things he would like to eat.

3 Match the highlighted words and phrases in the text with the meanings.

1 I get something from it, even though it's difficult. ....
2 give someone a job ....
3 with not much food ....
4 belonging to the past and the culture of a country ....
5 something that is difficult to do or learn ....
6 the way of life and beliefs that the people of a country share ....

SPEAKING

1 Write the words in the correct order to make expressions for starting a conversation and keeping it going.

1 name / what's / your

_____ ?

2 meet / nice / you / to

_____ .

3 from / you / where / are

_____ ?

4 you / do / what / do

_____ ?

5 you / are / how

_____ ?

6 like / you / to / music / listening / do

_____ ?

2 Match the answers with the questions and expressions in exercise 1.

a New York. It's a great city! ....

b It's Paul. ....

c Yes, I do. I love it! ....

d I'm fine, thanks. ....

e I'm a journalist. ....

f Nice to meet you, too. ....

3 Choose the correct responses.

1 I go running three times a week.
  A I agree. I like running, too.
  B Really? I like running, too.

2 Hi. My name's George.
  A Nice to meet you.
  B How are you?

3 I love cooking.
  A I am too.
  B Me too.

4 I'm a chef.
  A That sounds interesting.
  B I agree. Do you work in a restaurant?

5 I think the job of a police officer is very difficult.
  A Really? And it's dangerous, too.
  B I agree. It's quite dangerous, too.

6 I work in London.
  A Really? What do you do?
  B That sounds interesting. How are you?

WRITING

1 Complete the blog entry with the correct words and phrases (a–g).

Hello! **1**_____ and I'm 22. I'm Spanish and I live in Madrid. **2**_____ and I work for a big computer company. **3**_____! I usually get up at seven o'clock **4**_____. I get home at about seven in the evening **5**_____. Then I usually watch TV before I go to bed.
I love sport, especially football. **6**_____ and I also love watching sport on TV. **7**_____. I can make really good pizzas!

a and I start work at eight

b I play for a team in my town

c My name's Alejandro

d I also enjoy cooking

e and I prepare some food

f I'm a computer programmer

g Welcome to my blog

2 Read the first part of another blog entry. Find and correct six mistakes.

Hello! My name's Rob and I'm 18 year old. At the moment I'm study to become police officer. Welcome to my blog!
My classes start usually at nine o'clock, so I always get up early. I always am tired when I get home in the evenings. At the weekend I enjoy hang out with my friends, and we often go to the cinema together.

1 GETTING AWAY

VOCABULARY

1 Match the beginnings and ends of the sentences that Sofia says about her holiday activities.

1 I always feel excited when I'm packing ....
2 I love discovering ....
3 I don't spend much time just sunbathing by ....
4 I don't buy ....
5 I always take ....
6 I like hiking ....
7 It's nice to spend a day sightseeing ....
8 I always have fun playing ....
9 When I go to a new city, I prefer exploring on ....

a many souvenirs to take home with me.
b exciting new places when I'm on holiday.
c the pool or on the beach.
d games on the beach with friends.
e in the mountains if the weather's nice.
f lots of photos!
g my own, rather than going on a tour.
h in a new city and visiting all the tourist sites.
i my bags to go on holiday.

2 Choose the correct words to complete the sentences.

1 I think going on a long .... by train would be really boring!
   A transport   **B** journey   **C** travel
2 We're going on a ten-day .... to Morocco next month.
   A trip   **B** travel   **C** transport
3 Flying is not always the most expensive form of ....
   A tour   **B** transport   **C** trip
4 We went on a .... of the old city with a really interesting guide.
   A trip   **B** journey   **C** tour
5 I'd love to do a job that involves a lot of ....
   A travel   **B** transport   **C** journey

3 Complete the sentences with the correct weather words.

1 It's quite c .... today, so you might need a sweatshirt.
2 I hate it when the weather's grey and d .... !
3 What's the c .... m .... e like where you live?
4 I hate it when it rains and everything feels d .... p.
5 There was a storm last night, with lots of thunder and l .... t .... g.
6 It's warm here during the day, but it can be quite c .... y in the evening.

4 Choose the correct words to complete the online posts.

JJ44
I'm looking for somewhere to go on a hiking holiday in November. Any suggestions?

Marty_P
The island of Madeira is nice at that time of year. It's quite warm, with blue skies and plenty of ¹*sunshine / showers / climate*. It's a nice dry heat, too, so it doesn't feel too ²*dull / humid / mild*. Perfect!

SammyT33
I went to the Caribbean last year, but I wouldn't recommend it in November. It's the beginning of the wet season, so there may be frequent heavy ³*chilly / showers / damp*. It's also windy at that time of year too, so there may be a strong ⁴*lightning / breeze / dull*.

Suzy_S21
Why not go to Tenerife? It doesn't often rain there, so you can be fairly sure you'll get ⁵*fine / dull / damp* weather. Nights can be ⁶*mild / chilly / humid*, though, so take a few warm clothes with you.

GRAMMAR

1 Complete the advice about booking a holiday with the correct comparative or superlative form of the adjectives.

Booking a holiday?
Price isn't everything when you're booking a holiday, and the ¹ .... (cheap) holiday isn't necessarily the ² .... (good) one. For example, one hotel may cost less than another, but it may be a long way from the airport, so it's ³ .... (expensive) to get there by taxi. Also, a hotel that has low prices might have a ⁴ .... (small) pool than other hotels. This probably means the pool will be ⁵ .... (crowded) and not much fun! Many people choose the ⁶ .... (big) hotel they can find because they think this will have the ⁷ .... (comfortable) rooms. But this isn't always true, and big hotels are often ⁸ .... (noisy) than small ones. So, when you're looking for a holiday, don't just think about price – think about which holiday will be the ⁹ .... (enjoyable) for you.

2 Complete the second sentence so it has a similar meaning to the first. Use *less ...* or *(not) as ...* .

1 This hotel is older than the one near the beach.
The hotel near the beach _____ *isn't as old* as this one.

2 The beach was more crowded yesterday.
The beach is _____ today than it was yesterday.

3 This café is less expensive than the Italian one.
This café _____ as the Italian one.

4 This beach is beautiful, and the one we went to yesterday was beautiful too.
This beach is as _____ the one we went to yesterday.

5 This city isn't as interesting as I expected.
This city _____ than I expected.

3 Complete the holiday complaints with *too* or *enough* and the words in brackets.

1 The pool was _____ (cold) to swim in!

2 I guess our room was _____ (clean), but it wasn't nicely decorated.

3 There were lots of restaurants, but they were all _____ (expensive) for us.

4 Our balcony wasn't _____ (big) for us to sit on.

5 We only stayed for a few days, so we didn't have _____ (time) to do very much.

4 Complete the sentences with *so* or *such a*.

1 I'm _____ happy that I'm going on holiday tomorrow!

2 Why have you got _____ big bag?

3 Spain is _____ lovely country to visit!

4 It was _____ exciting going on the boat trip.

5 I'd love to go to Cuba, but it's _____ long way!

5 Choose the correct words to complete the email.

Hi Paula,

I'm having ¹*so / such / enough* a great time here in Ireland. The countryside is even ²*more / the most / as* beautiful than I expected, and the people here are ³*enough / such / so* friendly and welcoming. It isn't ⁴*less hot / hotter / as hot as* Spain, of course, but it's ⁵*too warm / so warm / warm enough* for hiking and sightseeing. Luckily, it hasn't been ⁶*such / more / too* wet – we've only had one day of rain! The ⁷*more / most / less* surprising thing is the food – it's amazing, and it's ⁸*so / less / as* expensive than I thought, which is good! The ⁹*bigger / too big / biggest* problem has been travelling around. The buses here are ¹⁰*cheaper / so cheap / not as cheap* than the trains, but there aren't many of them in the countryside, so I think we might need to hire a car.

See you when I get back,

Jan

Complete the words in the sentences.

1 Some parts of the world are getting much warmer because of c _____ m _____ e c _____ ge.

2 Plastic water bottles are definitely not e _____ r _____ m _____ t _____ y f _____ n _____ y!

3 Travelling by train rather than plane will reduce your c _____ b _____ n f _____ t _____ t.

4 We all need to recycle more so that we produce less w _____ e.

5 We should use clean forms of energy rather than burning f _____ s _____ l f _____ s.

6 It's important to support the c _____ s _____ v _____ n of the rainforest.

LISTENING

1 04 Listen to an interview on a holiday show. **What is the show about?**

A an unusual holiday on a cruise ship that costs a lot of money

B a competition in which someone can win a luxury holiday

C a holiday company that wants to pay someone to go on holiday

2 04 Listen to the interview again. Decide if the sentences are true or false.

1 The company wants someone to go on seven different holidays.

2 The person has to write a blog and upload photos to social media.

3 The person also has to upload a video, but they can't choose what it is about.

4 The person won't pay for their travel or food, and will also receive money to pay for souvenirs.

5 The company is employing this person to help advertise its holidays.

6 To apply, you should write to the company and send some of your holiday photos.

For each question, choose the correct answer.

The people below all want to find a hotel near the beach.
On the right there are eight hotels near the beach.
Decide which hotel would be most suitable for the people below.

1 Tanya wants a hotel directly on the beach so she can go for long walks. Apart from that, she doesn't plan to leave her hotel, so wants all meals and plenty of things to do there.

2 Susie wants to stay at a small quiet hotel. She wants the hotel to provide transport to a nearby town so that she can do lots of shopping there.

3 Rafael needs a hotel which provides suitable activities and food for young children. He also wants the hotel restaurant to serve a range of international food that he and his wife can enjoy.

4 Tommy is looking for a hotel with access to a gym and swimming pool. He also wants his hotel to be within walking distance of entertainment facilities for the evenings.

5 Angelica and her sister Katrin want a hotel which is next to a busy beach where they can take lessons in a watersport and go swimming in the sea.

HOLIDAY HOTELS

A LUXUS HOTEL
You never need to step outside this hotel as it has a full programme of activities for adults, from fitness classes and yoga to cooking lessons and garden tours. There's also a choice of four international restaurants to suit different tastes. The balcony has fantastic views over the town and the beach beyond.

B OCEAN VIEW
It's easy to visit the local attractions – a castle and a children's fun park – because the public bus stops outside the hotel entrance. Behind the hotel is a small beach which is often crowded with sunbathers and swimmers. There's also a diving and sailing school, where hotel guests can get a discount.

C SEASIDE HOTEL
This small, family-owned hotel offers fantastic home-cooked food. The hotel is only five minutes' walk to a busy beach but it's outside a town. If guests wish to go out in the evenings, it's better to bring your own car or hire one.

D GOLDEN SANDS HOTEL
This friendly hotel has a fantastic sports and entertainment programme to keep kids busy all day. There's only one restaurant but the menu changes daily, includes food from around the world and is suitable for all ages. There's an evening babysitting service so that adults can eat later.

E BLUE WAVES HOTEL
This busy hotel is ten minutes on foot to the town where there are discos and nightly concerts. The fitness centre's great for those who want to stay active on holiday, and guests can use the twenty-five-metre pool at the hotel next door. Free transport is provided to and from the airport.

F HARRY'S HOTEL
This hotel is right on the beach so guests can sit and watch surfers in the water. There are only twenty-five bedrooms so the atmosphere's always peaceful. All meals are provided and are cooked by a French chef. The town centre's great for buying gifts, clothes and shoes, and the hotel minibus takes guests there for free.

G DUNES HOTEL
This hotel, located away from the town, has everything you need, from a large swimming pool, games room and gym to clothes shops and a mini-supermarket. Breakfast and dinner are included, and it's possible to add lunch for a small charge. To reach the five-kilometre sandy beach, guests just need to cross the hotel garden.

H SUNSET HOTEL
A ten-minute taxi ride along the coast takes guests to a nearby town with a choice of watersports, including surfing and windsurfing lessons, as well as lively nightlife. The hotel has a private beach for sunbathing, but for swimming it's best to use the hotel pool.

SPEAKING

1 Read the phrases. Decide if each one is making a suggestion (S), asking for an opinion (O), agreeing (A) or disagreeing (D).

1 What do you think? ....
2 Sorry, but I don't agree. ....
3 Yes, you're right. ....
4 Perhaps they could visit a museum. ....
5 That's true. ....
6 Do you agree? ....
7 I think they should go to the beach. ....
8 Really? ....

2 Complete the conversations with the words in the box. There are two words you don't need.

afraid	agree	best	enjoy	great
might	opinion	really	think	

A: They ¹................ like a trip to the theatre.
B: Do you ²................ so? I'm not sure.

A: I think the ³................ way to get to Paris is by train.
B: I'm ⁴................ I disagree with you. The train is too slow.

A: I think they'd ⁵................ going shopping. What's your ⁶................?
B: I think that's a ⁷................ idea. Most people like shopping.

3 Choose the correct phrases in the conversations.

A: ¹*Perhaps they could / They might like* spend the day sightseeing.
B: ²*That's true. / Really?* I think that might be fun.

A: ³*I think they'd enjoy / I think they should* visiting the zoo.
B: ⁴*Do you agree? / Yes, you're right.* They'd like that.

A: I think a barbecue is the best idea for a meal. ⁵*What do you think? / Really?*
B: ⁶*I'm afraid I disagree with you. / Yes, you're right.* A barbecue isn't fun if it's raining.

4 Choose the best answer to each question.

1 Do you prefer to travel by plane or by train?
   A I'd rather go by plane because it's quicker.
   B Trains and planes are both expensive, but the train is usually a bit cheaper.

2 What do you think about organised tours?
   A I sometimes go on organised tours, but I usually explore new cities on my own.
   B I think organised tours can be interesting sometimes, if you're in a new city.

3 Would you rather spend a day sunbathing or sightseeing?
   A I love sunbathing, and I also like sightseeing because it's interesting.
   B I'd prefer to go sightseeing for the day because I think it's more interesting.

4 What's the best time of year for you to go on holiday?
   A I think the spring is my favourite time to go on holiday because it isn't as busy as the summer.
   B The summer is usually too expensive for some people, so a lot of people prefer the autumn.

5 Do you enjoy hiking in the mountains?
   A There are lots of great mountains in my country, and a lot of people go hiking there.
   B Yes, I love hiking in the mountains because you can get some amazing views from the top.

WRITING

1 Choose the correct linking words.

1 *Although / But* the beach was crowded, there was enough space for us to find a place to relax.
2 The city centre has some beautiful old buildings. *What's more, / As well,* there are also some amazing shops.
3 The hotel has two swimming pools, and tennis courts *also / too.*
4 The food was excellent, *and / but* the waiters were all very friendly.
5 *As well as / Also* visiting the museum, we also had time for lunch in a small café.
6 The train journey was long, *what's more / but* we didn't mind because the scenery was beautiful.

2 Complete the sentences with the linking words in the box.

also	although
and	as well as
though	too

1 A helicopter trip is a great way to see the city, ... it doesn't cost too much.
2 The old city centre is lovely, and the castle is .... worth a visit.
3 .... we were tired, we decided to go for a walk along the beach.
4 .... being very crowded, the museum was old-fashioned and not very interesting.
5 The park is a great place to relax. There's a very good café there, ...
6 We had an amazing holiday. It was very expensive, ...

2 ENTERTAIN ME

VOCABULARY

Read the clues and complete the puzzle with the correct entertainment words. Use the shaded letters to make an extra word.

1	S			D	T				
2	B			S				R	
3	A					E			
4	T				R				
5	E		S						
6	C								
7	S								

1 the music that plays during a film
2 a very popular book that a lot of people buy
3 the people who watch a play or show
4 a very exciting film or book
5 one part of a TV series
6 a funny film that makes you laugh
7 the part of a theatre where the actors stand to perform

Extra word: d_____

Clue: It might be about animals.

GRAMMAR

1 Complete the text with the present perfect or past simple form of the verbs.

Nearly a star!

Do you want to be a star? I ¹_____ (never / be) interested in being on TV, but last year a friend of mine ²_____ (go) to an event to find good singers for a talent show. He ³_____ (always / love) singing, so it ⁴_____ (seem) perfect for him. He ⁵_____ (sing) well for the judges, and they ⁶_____ (accept) him onto the show. He's really excited because he ⁷_____ (not do) anything like this before. As for me, I ⁸_____ (never / see) a friend of mine on TV before, so I can't wait to watch the show!

2 Write the questions using the present perfect or past simple form of the verbs. Then complete the short answers.

1 **A:** you / enjoy / the concert / last Saturday?
   _____?
   B: Yes, I _____. It was amazing!

2 **A:** you / ever / act / in a play?
   _____?
   B: Yes, I _____. But I don't think I was very good!

3 **A:** you / go / to / any festivals / last summer?
   _____?
   B: No, I _____. But I'd like to go to some this year.

4 **A:** Paul / see / the new *Star Wars* film yet?
   _____?
   B: Yes, he _____. He loved it!

5 **A:** Freya / win / the singing competition / last week?
   _____?
   B: Yes, she _____. She's a really good singer!

6 **A:** your friends / ever / organise / a surprise party for you?
   _____?
   B: No, they _____, but I organised one for a friend of mine recently.

3 Complete the second sentence so it has the same meaning as the first. Use *for* or *since*.

1 I started at this college in 2019.
   I've been at this ....
   2019.

2 Ollie started work at the café three months ago.
   Ollie has worked at ....
   three months.

3 My brother got this tablet last year.
   My brother has had this ....
   last year.

4 I first met Laura five years ago.
   I've known .... five years.

5 Hana became interested in dance when she was five.
   Hana has been interested ....
   she was five.

6 My grandparents started living in this house a long time ago.
   My grandparents have lived in ....
   a long time.

4 Complete the conversation with *yet* and *already*.

A: Have you seen the latest episode of *Secret Lives*
   ¹ .... ?

B: No, I haven't. I know it's on catch-up TV, but I haven't had time to watch it ² ....
   But I've ³ .... decided that it was David who killed Magda.

A: Really? I think there are a few possibilities.

B: Yes, but the police have ⁴ .... found a few things that show it's David.

A: Hmm, but they haven't arrested him ⁵ .... ,
   so I'm not sure. Freddie says there are some spoilers online – have you read any of them ⁶ .... ?

B: No, and I don't want to – I'm happy to wait and see what happens!

5 Complete the text with the correct form of *used to* and the verbs in brackets.

In the early days of film-making things
¹ .... (be) very different for the actors. Firstly, they ² .... (not speak) in the films, because there was no sound. Someone ³ .... (play) the piano in cinemas while the audience watched the film. And how ⁴ .... (they / do) dangerous things, like in this photo? Nowadays, film makers can use computers to make things look exciting, or they use special actors to do the dangerous scenes. But in the 1920s that ⁵ .... (not happen). The main actors ⁶ .... (perform) in every scene, even when it was dangerous!

LISTENING PART 2

🔊 05 **For each question, choose the correct answer.**

1 You will hear two friends talking about a film they have just seen.
   What does the woman say?
   A The film was too long.
   B The story was hard to follow.
   C The main actor was disappointing.

2 You will hear a brother and sister talking about booking concert tickets.
   They agree to book seats
   A near the stage.
   B at the side.
   C in the balcony.

3 You will hear a woman telling a friend about a TV programme.
   What type of programme did she watch?
   A a soap opera
   B a crime series
   C a documentary

4 You will hear two people talking about online newspapers.
   Why does the man prefer online newspapers to TV news?
   A They are more suitable for his busy lifestyle.
   B They focus on more interesting topics.
   C They provide more detailed information.

5 You will hear a man telling a friend about a play called *The Visit*.
   How does he feel?
   A satisfied that he has seen it
   B impressed by the way that it ended
   C excited about the director's next play

6 You will hear two friends talking about a summer music festival.
   One thing the woman likes about the festival is that
   A it isn't too crowded.
   B tickets aren't too expensive.
   C travelling there isn't too difficult.

1 Read the article. How does it answer the question in the title below? Choose the best answer.

A Not many people knew about superheroes in the past, but now more people know about them.

B The use of computers has made superhero films more realistic, so now more people can enjoy them.

C Film makers now use better stories in superhero films, so they are more exciting.

Everyone is suddenly crazy about superhero films! Recent films like *Black Panther, The Avengers* and *Thor* have become popular all over the world. But why? Most of the characters are not new. They have been in stories in comics since the 1960s. So why are superhero films suddenly so popular now?

One reason is that the basic superhero story is very simple and familiar. We would all love to be a superhero – a normal person who gets amazing magic powers. We can imagine that suddenly we are super-strong or can run super-fast, or fly through the air. We then use these powers to fight a bad guy who wants to destroy the world, and everyone loves us! Wonderful!

These stories worked well in comics. Artists made simple drawings of Spiderman climbing up walls or Superman flying above the city. Our imagination did the rest. But with superhero films in the past, this didn't work. The audience couldn't believe the story they were watching. They could see that the superheroes weren't *really* flying, or climbing up walls. They just looked like normal people in rather silly clothes!

But this has all changed. Budgets are much bigger and films are much better than they used to be. The costumes actors wear now are amazing. But there's something more important. Film makers now use computers to make the superheroes *look* real. When we see Superman flying, we can now *believe* that he is flying.

Because the stories now *look* real on the screen, we can enjoy them again, like we did in the comics. Our imagination can take control again. We can believe there really *is* a superhero, and he (or she) really *can* save the world! At the same time, we can enjoy the amazing pictures, the soundtrack and the excellent acting.

Fans have waited for a long time to see good superhero films. But they are finally here. Now not just children, but old and young alike, can escape into these imaginary worlds. With the help of computers and amazing special effects, everyone can really enjoy these simple stories of magic and power, and good defeating bad.

WHY DO WE SUDDENLY LOVE SUPERHEROES?

2 Read the article again. Choose the correct answers.

1 Most of the characters in superhero films *have changed / haven't changed* since the 1960s.

2 Most people *can imagine they are / wouldn't like to* be a superhero.

3 Audiences thought the first film superheroes *were amazing / looked disappointing*.

4 It is easier to enjoy superhero films now because *they look more like the stories in comics / they look more realistic*.

5 *Especially young people / People of all ages* now enjoy superhero films.

PUSH YOURSELF / B2

Choose the correct phrasal verbs to complete the sentences.

1 I used to be good friends with Ali, but I _____ with him last year.

2 My brother has really _____ tennis recently – he loves it!

3 You shouldn't worry about things so much – you should _____ more!

4 Henry was really upset when his band _____ last year.

5 I think if you enjoy acting, you should _____ doing it – don't listen to anyone else!

6 My parents always want me to do well, and I don't want to _____.

7 A local café offered me a part-time job, but I _____.

8 Ben's dad is a famous actor, so Ben feels he has to _____.

1	**A** fell out	**B** chilled out	**C** kept on
2	**A** turned down	**B** got into	**C** lived up to
3	**A** keep on	**B** split up	**C** chill out
4	**A** let down	**B** split up	**C** kept on
5	**A** keep on	**B** fall out	**C** turn down
6	**A** turn them down	**B** get into them	**C** let them down
7	**A** fell out	**B** turned it down	**C** split up with them
8	**A** let him down	**B** fall out with him	**C** live up to him

SPEAKING

Complete the conversations with the words in the box. There are two words you don't need.

crazy	enjoy	fan	into	mind
stand	bothered	thing		

1 **A:** We could watch a film on your phone.

B: No. I can't _____ watching films on my phone – the screen's far too small!

2 **A:** Do you want to go bowling later?

B: No, I don't like bowling – it isn't my _____ .

3 **A:** Did you enjoy that film?

B: Yes. I'm not usually a _____ of romantic films, but this one was quite good.

4 **A:** Does your sister like that new band, New Day?

B: Yes, they're her favourite band now. She's completely _____ about them!

5 **A:** Have you heard the new song by Tamara?

B: Yes, it's great. I'm really _____ her music.

6 **A:** Where do you want to sit?

B: Well, I don't _____ sitting near the back of the cinema, but I'd prefer to be nearer the front.

WRITING

1 Complete the beginnings and endings for emails with the words in the box.

Bye	Dear	Hi (x2)	Looking	See	to seeing

Email beginnings:

1 _____ ,

2 _____ Anna,

3 _____ Anna,

Email endings:

4 _____ for now.

5 _____ you soon.

6 _____ forward _____ you.

2 We often use short forms in informal emails. Write one short form for each sentence.

1 There is a concert next Saturday. ___There's___

2 Where is the festival taking place? _____

3 I will get the tickets. _____

4 I would love to come with you. _____

5 That is a really nice idea. _____

6 Jack is coming to the concert with us. _____

3 Choose the correct words in the messages.

Hi Lucas,
¹_Would / Do_ you like to come for a pizza with me tonight? We **²**_could / may_ meet in town, if you like.
Hope you can come!
Sam

Hi Sam,
Thanks for the invitation. **³**_Sorry, but / No, but_ I have to revise tonight because I've got exams tomorrow. How about **⁴**_go / going_ tomorrow night instead?
Bye for now,
Lucas

Hi Lucas,
⁵_That sounds / That's_ a nice idea. Let's **⁶**_meet / meeting_ at seven o'clock. Why **⁷**_we don't / don't we_ ask Kallum to come too?
Looking forward to seeing you,
Sam

4 Look at the sentences in exercise 3. Are they suggestions, invitations or responses? Write S, I or R.

1 _____		*3* _____		*5* _____		*7* _____
2 _____		*4* _____		*6* _____		

3 DINING OUT, EATING IN

VOCABULARY

1 Unjumble the letters in brackets to complete what Laura says about a meal. Then use the shaded letters to answer the question below.

> I had a **1**_____ (lema) in an Italian restaurant last night, with some friends. I had a **2**_____ (lowb) of really nice soup first, as a **3**_____ (artster). I couldn't decide which **4**_____ (hisd) to have for my main **5**_____ (croseu). In the end I had fish. It was nice, but there was too much food on my **6**_____ (lapet) and I couldn't finish it all. I did manage some ice cream for dessert, though! When the **7**_____ (lilb) came, I was surprised because it wasn't too expensive. We left a big **8**_____ (pti) for the waiter, because he was really helpful.

Which part of the meal did Laura enjoy the most?
d _____ _____ _____ _____

2 Choose the correct words to complete the comments about a new restaurant.

> You should definitely try this restaurant. It **1**_____ really good food!

> Excellent food, but quite busy, so you need to **2**_____ a table before you go.

> We don't often **3**_____ out for dinner, but we thought we'd try it. We weren't disappointed!

> The waiter was really friendly when he **4**_____ us to our table.

> It was a bit slow. We waited quite a long time for the waiter to **5**_____ us the menu.

> Very helpful waitress. She **6**_____ our coats and helped us choose what to eat.

> We **7**_____ our food at 7.30 and didn't eat until 8.30!

> Very expensive. When I **8**_____ for the bill, I couldn't believe how much it was!!

1	**A** gives	**B** serves	**C** brings
2	**A** choose	**B** keep	**C** reserve
3	**A** go	**B** take	**C** spend
4	**A** asked	**B** showed	**C** put
5	**A** take	**B** carry	**C** bring
6	**A** lifted	**B** removed	**C** took
7	**A** ordered	**B** asked	**C** demanded
8	**A** invited	**B** offered	**C** asked

3 Choose the correct words to complete the recipe.

Pasta with mushroom sauce

Chop some onions and garlic into small pieces, and slice the mushrooms. **1**Fry / Grate / Grill these for a few minutes in a large pan, in a small amount of oil. **2**Pour / Add / Mix salt and pepper and some fresh herbs, and a little cream. **3**Grate / Mix / Grill everything together in the pan, and **4**add / heat / slice gently for a few minutes. Meanwhile, boil some pasta in water. To serve, **5**mix / put / slice the pasta onto the plate and **6**heat / pour / mix the mushroom sauce over the pasta. **7**Fry / Grate / Heat a little cheese over the top. Delicious!

GRAMMAR

1 Choose the correct modifier in the sentences.

1 Mmm, this soup tastes very / absolutely delicious!
2 Those biscuits look quite / absolutely nice.
3 That fish smells really / absolutely good.
4 Those desserts look extremely / absolutely gorgeous!
5 Ooh, this ice cream is extremely / absolutely tasty!
6 I'm sorry, but that smells very / really disgusting!

2 Choose the correct word to complete the sentences.

1 Shall I add a _____ salt to the soup? (few / little)
2 There isn't _____ ice cream in the freezer. (any / no)
3 There are a _____ biscuits left. Would you like one? (few / little)
4 There isn't _____ milk in the fridge. (many / much)
5 There are _____ onions in this recipe. (any / no)

3 Complete the conversations with words from the box. There is one word you don't need.

a	an	any	few	little
lot	many	much	some	

A: How **1**_____ apples do we need for this recipe?
B: We only need a **2**_____ – just two or three, I think.

A: Would you like **3**_____ coffee?
B: No thanks. I don't drink **4**_____ coffee – just one cup in the morning.

A: I'm thirsty. Is there **5**_____ apple juice in the fridge?
B: No, but there's a **6**_____ orange juice. Would you like that?

A: We've got a **7**_____ of eggs in the fridge. Shall I make **8**_____ omelette for lunch?
B: Yes, that would be lovely!

4 Complete the second sentence so it has the same meaning as the first.

1 We don't have many eggs.
We only have _____ eggs.

2 There's no cake left!
There isn't _____ cake left!

3 I don't usually add much salt when I'm cooking.
I don't usually add a _____ of salt when I'm cooking.

4 There isn't much coffee in the jar.
There's only _____ coffee in the jar.

5 I don't have a lot of recipe books.
I only have _____ recipe books.

5 Complete the sentences with *a, an, the* or *Ø* (zero article).

1 Do you like _____ strawberries?
2 I need _____ glass of water.
3 Where's _____ cake that I bought yesterday?
4 Would you like _____ orange?
5 I don't usually have _____ sugar in my coffee.
6 Can you put _____ milk back in the fridge, please?
7 She's a vegetarian, so she doesn't eat _____ meat.
8 Would you like _____ slice of bread?

6 Choose the correct words to complete the blog post.

As you know, I love writing about **¹**some / Ø / the food. I don't go to **²**the / many / lot restaurants, so when **³**a / the / any friend invited me to **⁴**a / an / Ø new Spanish restaurant called El Sabor, I said yes immediately. It was fantastic! There were **⁵**much / the / a lot of really delicious dishes to choose from, and **⁶**the / Ø / much desserts were amazing! If you go, you must try **⁷**Ø / the / some fish dish with chips and lemon. My only complaint was that they didn't bring us **⁸**some / a / any bread to eat with our meal.

LISTENING

1 🎧 06 **Listen to the first part of an interview with Elsa, a food journalist, about a restaurant in New York. What is different about this restaurant?**

A All the cooks are grandmothers.
B The people who cook are all training to be chefs.
C You don't have to pay for the food.

2 🎧 07 **Listen to the rest of the interview and choose the correct answers.**

1 How did Elsa learn about this restaurant?
A A friend told her about it.
B She read a review of it online.
C She drove past an advertisement for it.

2 Mr Scaravella started the restaurant because
A he was fed up with eating in expensive restaurants.
B he wanted to remember his own grandmother's food.
C he wanted to encourage people to eat out more.

3 What do we learn about the menu?
A All the dishes are completely different every night.
B There are dishes from a different country every night.
C Some of the dishes are not very popular.

4 The different women who cook at the restaurant
A all compete with each other to make the best dishes.
B don't like tasting each other's food.
C give each other new ideas for cooking.

5 What do we learn about the cooking classes at the restaurant?
A You don't have to book in advance.
B They are free.
C They are only for women.

6 What did Elsa most enjoy about the experience?
A the food
B the atmosphere
C talking to other guests

Five sentences have been removed from the text below.

For each question, choose the correct answer.

There are three extra sentences which you do not need to use.

SWEETS – an ancient product

In a cave near Valencia in Spain there are paintings of people climbing trees to collect and eat the honey from bees' nests. Experts have studied these and reached the conclusion that they are eight thousand years old. **(1)** ＿＿＿＿＿ And that's not hard to understand because, for most people today, eating sweets is a very enjoyable thing to do.

The next time that sweet foods appear in history is around four thousand years ago in India. We know this from ancient texts that were written at that time in the Sanskrit language. **(2)** ＿＿＿＿＿ Sadly though, no-one knows exactly what they tasted like. We also know that the ancient Egyptians, Greeks and Romans all loved sweets, which they made by rolling fruit or nuts in honey. However, we now know that sugar was available in ancient Rome. **(3)** ＿＿＿＿＿ For this reason, sugar wasn't used for making sweets but for adding to medicines.

In Europe in the Middle Ages (the 6th–16th centuries) the price of sugar meant that only very rich people could afford sweets. **(4)** ＿＿＿＿＿ They could earn lots of money from having their own shop or from working in the palaces of kings and queens. Sweets were made by hand using boiled sugar or an ingredient called marzipan. It was common at the time to create sculptures of animals, castles, trees and even people. Some of the sculptures were huge and were presented to guests at formal dinners.

The kinds of sweets we recognise today were first made in the nineteenth century. The development of factories meant that sweets could be made in very large quantities. **(5)** ＿＿＿＿＿ The kinds of things they were able to buy were boiled sweets, chewing gum, toffee and chocolate.

A   Sweet-makers were considered to be highly skilled professionals.

B   Sugar comes from a plant which is known as sugarcane.

C   These pictures show that people in ancient times loved eating sweet things.

D   People believed this ingredient could cure various illnesses.

E   Chocolate from Central America came to Europe in the 1500s.

F   They have a lovely taste and give us lots of energy.

G   This affected the price, and sweets became popular with ordinary people.

H   The documents describe sweets which were made using milk and sugar.

PUSH YOURSELF B2

1 Write the words in the correct order to make idioms.

1 piece / it's / cake / a / of

_____

2 cup / not / of / tea / my / it's

_____

3 pinch / take / salt / of / it / a / with / I'd

_____

4 beans / he / the / spilt

_____

5 all / pear-shaped / gone / it's

_____

6 spilt / good / milk / no / it's / crying / over

_____

2 Decide which idiom from exercise 1 could replace what each person said.

a It's happened and you can't change it now, so it's not worth worrying about it. _____

b It's really easy! _____

c Everything's gone wrong! _____

d He told them all about it! _____

e You definitely shouldn't believe that! _____

f I don't like that kind of thing. _____

SPEAKING

1 Look at the photo and choose the correct words to complete the text.

I can see a family. I'm ¹*not sure / not being sure*, but I think they're in a café, because there are spoons and forks on the table ²*behind / in front of* the glasses. There's a boy ³*in / on* the left. He ⁴*holds / is holding* something. I don't know what it is. It looks ⁵*as / like* a menu, or maybe a book. I think it's summer ⁶*so / because* they're wearing summer clothes, and the man ⁷*at / in* the back of the photo is wearing a sun hat.

2 Match the beginnings and ends of the sentences for talking about photographs.

1	This is a photo	**a**	a cake on the table.
2	There's	**b**	they're called.
3	I can	**c**	of a café.
4	I don't know what	**d**	for serving water.
5	People use them	**e**	like a large jug.
6	She's holding something. It looks	**f**	see four people.

WRITING

1 Complete the time expressions in the sentences with the correct words. There are three words you don't need.

after	at	end	finish	last
later	past	then	when	

1 I went out for a meal _____ weekend.

2 _____ the waiter arrived, she seemed very friendly.

3 _____ first, the food tasted a bit strange.

4 _____ a while, I started to enjoy it.

5 At the _____ of the meal, I felt very happy.

6 Our food arrived half an hour _____.

2 Choose the correct time expressions in the story.

I invited some friends to my flat for a meal ¹*after a while / last Saturday*. I like cooking, so I was happy to cook a meal for everyone. ²*When they arrived / Next*, we sat down at the table and I brought the food out. We started eating, but ³*at first / then* everyone started coughing. There was too much pepper in the food! I brought some water, but it was no good. ⁴*After a while / At the end of the meal*, we decided that we really couldn't eat it. I was a bit upset ⁵*at first / next*, but then I saw the funny side of it. ⁶*Next / At first*, we had to decide what to do! We decided to order some pizzas, and we had a great evening together. ⁷*At the end of the evening / Then they left*, everyone thanked me and went home. I'm sure we'll continue to laugh about it for a long time!

4 CITY LIVING?

VOCABULARY

1 Write the words next to the definitions. There are two words you don't need.

| apartment block | nature | neighbourhood |
| scenery | skyscraper | stream | valley | waterfall |

1 a small river ....
2 the area where you live ....
3 a large building with lots of flats in it
  ....
4 water that falls from high up ....
5 a very tall building ....
6 an area of low land between two mountains
  ....

2 Complete the words in the sentences.

1 It was easy to get around the city because there were lots of s_____ np_____ts showing us where things were.
2 The quickest way to travel across New York is to use the s_____ _____y.
3 Let's buy a burger from the f_____ t_____ k over there.
4 The city has an amazing sk_____ne, with lots of tall buildings.
5 I love spending time outdoors with n_____e all around me.
6 When we got to the top of the hill we stopped to enjoy the beautiful sc_____y around us.

3 Read what the people say about the places. Match the adjectives with what the people say.

1 A lot of great and interesting things happen here! ....
2 It's always quiet here. ....
3 The people are very kind here. ....
4 Nothing ever happens here! ....
5 This place looks really lovely. ....
6 It's never quiet here! ....

| a | beautiful | c | exciting | e | friendly |
| b | noisy | d | peaceful | f | boring |

GRAMMAR

1 Complete the text with the past simple or past continuous form of the verbs.

It ¹........................ (rain) when I ²........................ (arrive) at Jo's apartment block, so I quickly ³........................ (run) up to the first floor and ⁴........................ (ring) the doorbell. While I ⁵........................ (wait) for Jo to open the door, I ⁶........................ (check) my phone. Yes, it was the right day and time for the party. I was surprised when there was no answer. While I ⁷........................ (think) about what to do, I ⁸........................ (see) another friend arriving. 'Hi,' I said. 'Jo's not in.' 'But you're at the wrong flat,' he said. 'Jo lives on the second floor.'

2 Join the sentences using *when* or *while*.

1 I was having a shower. The taxi arrived.
  The taxi ....
  ....
2 Tom was waiting for the bus. He saw Sam.
  Tom ....
  ....
3 Lia was living in London. She met Paul.
  Lia ....
  ....

3 Complete the sentences with the past perfect form of the verbs.

1 The film .... (already / start) when we got to the cinema.
2 Max .... (just / leave) the house when I called.
3 I was excited because I .... (never / try) waterskiing before.
4 .... (you / ever / visit) the United States before you went to study there?

4 Complete the text with the past simple or past perfect form of the verbs.

I ¹........................ (go) to Rome last summer. I ²........................ (never visit) Italy before, so I was really excited, and I wasn't disappointed! The ancient buildings ³........................ (look) amazing! I ⁴........................ (find) it hard to believe that people ⁵........................ (build) them so long ago, without any modern machines! We ⁶........................ (have) some great pizzas, and I was really pleased because I ⁷........................ (learn) a few phrases in Italian before I went, and I ⁸........................ (manage) to use them while I was there.

READING

1 Read the article about green skyscrapers. What does the article discuss? Choose the best answer.

  A the reasons why green skyscrapers are still not very popular
  B the advantages and disadvantages of green skyscrapers
  C the experiences of people who live in green skyscrapers

The country in the city?

Cities are often noisy and dirty places, and many people prefer the peaceful atmosphere of the countryside, with open fields and forests. However, there are many good reasons to live in cities – jobs, exciting things to do and plenty of new people to meet. Some architects are now trying to bring the country into the city by creating 'green skyscrapers'.

The Bosco Verticale in Milan is a skyscraper which tries to create a 'forest in the sky'. It opened in 2014 and has two towers, one just over 100 metres high and the other around 80 metres high. Inside, it is mainly apartments, but there are also some offices. The special thing about this skyscraper is that there are nearly 1,000 trees, and also hundreds of smaller plants, growing all over it.

Skyscrapers like this are more difficult and more expensive to build. There are problems with planting trees so high up – not all kinds of trees can live in the strong winds at this height. Also, someone has to look after the plants, to water them in hot weather and cut them back when they grow too big, so they don't spoil the view for the people who live there. This could be a lot of work for the people who live there, but at Bosco Verticale, a special team of professional gardeners takes care of it.

But green skyscrapers also bring a lot of benefits. The trees and plants clean the air, keep the apartments cool in hot weather and reduce the amount of noise that people hear inside the building. More importantly, most people would agree that they are much more attractive to look at than the usual metal and glass. Some architects believe that over the next 20 years green buildings could change the skyline of our cities, to make them look more like forests.

I visited Singapore recently, and stayed in the Parkroyal on Pickering hotel. This 'hotel in a garden' is a great example of a green skyscraper. The building is covered in plants, and there is a 'skygarden', where guests can sit and enjoy views of the city. There are plants everywhere, and I was amazed that there are even indoor waterfalls! Rooms aren't cheap, but the price is worth paying to get the chance to escape from the noise and dirt outside and enjoy a little bit of the countryside in the heart of the city.

2 Read the article again. Choose the correct answers.

1 In the first paragraph, what does the writer say about cities?
  A Most people find cities too noisy and dirty.
  B There are a lot of benefits to living in cities.
  C There are too many new buildings in cities.

2 What do we learn about Bosco Verticale?
  A There are more than two towers.
  B There are only apartments inside.
  C It has trees and other plants growing on it.

3 Why are some trees not suitable to use in green skyscrapers?
  A They don't like the weather conditions.
  B They are too expensive.
  C They need too much water in hot weather.

4 What do we learn about the plants at Bosco Verticale?
  A They often cause problems when they get too big.
  B People are paid to look after them.
  C The people who live there find it difficult to look after them.

5 According to the writer, what is the biggest advantage of green skyscrapers?
  A They keep the apartments cool.
  B They reduce pollution.
  C They look nicer than other buildings.

6 How did the writer feel about staying in the Parkroyal on Pickering hotel?
  A disappointed at the views from the skygarden
  B surprised that there are waterfalls inside the hotel
  C angry about the high prices

08 **For each question, choose the correct answer.**

1 Where will the woman go camping this summer?

A  B  C

2 What's the view from the apartment block?

A  B  C

3 Which activity did the woman help with?

A  B  C

4 Where will the friends meet before going to the theatre?

A  B  C

5 Where is the problem in the apartment building?

A  B  C

6 What did the woman do in the park?

A  B  C

7 Where in the city will they eat tonight?

A  B  C

PUSH YOURSELF B2

Choose the correct verb forms to complete the text.

Last summer, my aunt and uncle ¹*took / were taking / had taken* me for a walk in the countryside while I ²*stayed / was staying / had stayed* with them. It was terrible! First, my feet ³*got / were getting / had got* wet because I ⁴*didn't bring / wasn't bringing / hadn't brought* any strong shoes with me. Then some cows ⁵*ran / were running / had run* after us while we ⁶*walked / were walking / had walked* through a field. Finally, we ⁷*spent / were spending / had spent* hours trying to find our way back because my uncle ⁸*forgot / was forgetting / had forgotten* to bring the map with him. I think I'll stay in the city this year!

SPEAKING

1 Complete the conversations with the words in the box.

about	better	could	idea	let's
like	shall	sounds	sure	that's

A: What do you want to do today?

B: What ¹_____ going to the park? There's a concert there this afternoon.

A: That ²_____ good.

A: ³_____ we go to the beach this afternoon?

B: I'm not ⁴_____. It isn't very warm!

A: It's a lovely evening. We ⁵_____ have a barbecue!

B: That's a nice ⁶_____. I'll invite some friends.

A: Yes, ⁷_____ great!

A: ⁸_____ go shopping today.

B: I don't really ⁹_____ that idea. I don't like shopping. There's a good film on at the cinema, though.

A: Yes, OK. I think that's a ¹⁰_____ idea.

2 Choose the correct response.

1 We could go for a pizza if you like.
- **A** Yes, I like.
- **B** That sounds good.
- **C** Shall we go?

2 What about watching a movie tonight?
- **A** That was great.
- **B** No, I don't want.
- **C** I think that's a great idea.

3 We could go ice skating.
- **A** I don't think that's a better idea.
- **B** Yes, what about it?
- **C** Hmm, I don't really like that idea.

4 Let's meet at 7.30.
- **A** That looks good.
- **B** Yes, that's great.
- **C** I don't really like 7.30.

5 Shall we organise a party?
- **A** I'm not sure.
- **B** That's good.
- **C** I love that!

6 What about buying Anna some earrings for her birthday?
- **A** Yes, let's buy.
- **B** No, we couldn't.
- **C** That's a nice idea.

WRITING

1 Complete the sentences with the words in the box. There is one word you don't need.

after	end	first	later	next	when	while

1 We walked round the shops all afternoon, and the _____ day, my feet really hurt!

2 We visited the art gallery and _____ that we went for a coffee.

3 I was really worried, but in the _____ everything was fine.

4 At _____ I thought Freddie was joking, but then I realised he was serious.

5 I saw Sara again _____, at the sports centre.

6 I was walking home _____ I suddenly noticed I didn't have my bag with me.

2 Choose the correct time linkers in the story.

It was my birthday on Saturday. ¹*While / At first* I was getting dressed in the morning, the doorbell rang. I opened the door and saw a big group of my friends. 'We're taking you out,' they said. We went for a coffee first, and ²*then / at first* we went to a big theme park near the town. We spent a few hours there, having a great time, and ³*when / after that* we went back into town for something to eat. ⁴*Later / When*, we all went back to one friend's flat and we watched a movie together. I was really tired but happy when I ⁵*in the end / finally* got home. It was an amazing day.

VOCABULARY

1 Read the clues and complete the puzzle. Then use the shaded letters to complete the sentence.

1 It's all over your body.
2 You bend it if you want to jump.
3 The femur is the longest one in your body.
4 You use it when you breathe.
5 You move it when you wave your hand.
6 It joins your foot to your leg.
7 If you lift heavy things, it will get bigger and stronger.
8 You can't talk without it.
9 It's at the top of your arm.

1		K				
2			E			
3		O				
4				G		
5					T	
6			K			
7				C		
8			N			
9					L	

10 Anna fell and hurt her ___ ___ ___ ___ ___ .

2 Complete what Marco says about his health.

I feel really ¹i _____ today. I think I've got a bad ²c _____ d. I've got a terrible ³s _____ e t _____ t, so I can't eat or drink anything, and I've also got a ⁴c _____ h, which gets worse every time I speak. I've got ⁵e _____ e in both my ears, and I can't walk around very much because I've got ⁶b _____ k _____ e! The only thing I can really do comfortably is lie on my bed and play computer games!

3 Choose the correct words to complete the sentences.

1 Be careful, or you'll *injury / injure / pain* yourself.
2 What happened to your arm? Is it *pain / pains / painful*?
3 Don't lift that heavy box – you might *sore / hurt / injury* your back.
4 My arm is really *pain / injury / sore* from falling off my bike.
5 I think you should go to the hospital – that looks like a serious *hurt / sore / injury*.

4 Complete the notice with the words in the box.

emergency	infection	patients
prescription	tablets	

Important notice

If you have an appointment with the doctor, please wait in the waiting area. There may be other ¹_____ before you, so please wait until your name is called. If the doctor gives you a ²_____, you can collect your medicines at the chemist's on Broad Street. Children are usually given liquid medicines but if you would prefer ³_____ for your child, please tell the doctor. If you are seriously ill and think the situation is an ⁴_____, please speak to the receptionist and she will call an ambulance. If you have an ⁵_____ which might be dangerous to other people, please do NOT come to the clinic. Call us, and we will arrange for the doctor to visit you at home.

GRAMMAR

1 Complete the second sentence so it has a similar meaning to the first. Use the correct form of the word in brackets.

1 I wasn't able to dive when I was younger.
I _____ when I was younger. (can)
2 I was able to ski when I was six!
I _____ when I was six! (can)
3 My baby cousin can walk now!
My baby cousin _____ now. (able)
4 I couldn't finish the race.
I _____ the race. (able)
5 My grandma isn't able to run marathons any more.
My grandma _____ marathons any more. (can)

2 Choose the correct words to complete the sentences.

1 You should *do / to do* more exercise.
2 I think you *ought to / ought* go to bed earlier.
3 You shouldn't *eating / eat* so much chocolate.
4 I don't think you *ought to / don't ought to* spend so much time playing on your computer.
5 You *shouldn't / don't ought to* drink so many sweet drinks.

3 Choose the correct words to complete the online posts.

Abi44G
I want to get fit quickly. I'm really unfit at the moment, and I **¹____** even run for a bus! I **²____** get to a gym because there isn't one near my house. Any ideas?

MaxPP
You **³____** start slowly and build up your fitness over a few months. Try walking to start with, and soon you **⁴____** run!

SamT99
You **⁵____** worry about not being near a gym. There's lots of gym equipment that you **⁶____** use at home, and it isn't expensive if you buy second-hand. Stop making excuses!

FitAmy
You definitely **⁷____** get a bike. I **⁸____** even ride a bike six months ago, but now I cycle everywhere, and it's a really great way to get fit!

1	**A** can't	**B** couldn't	**C** should
2	**A** ought to	**B** 'm not able to	**C** shouldn't
3	**A** couldn't	**B** ought	**C** should
4	**A** can	**B** were able to	**C** 'll be able to
5	**A** shouldn't	**B** could	**C** ought to
6	**A** can	**B** aren't able to	**C** shouldn't
7	**A** ought to	**B** can't	**C** were able to
8	**A** can't	**B** weren't able to	**C** couldn't

4 Complete the gym rules with the correct verbs. There is one verb you don't need.

don't need to book	don't have to bring	have to ask
must have	mustn't book	mustn't use	need to know

GYM RULES

1   All members ____
their membership cards with them at all times.

2   You ____
classes in advance, but it is a good idea for popular classes.

3   Junior members under 14 ____
the pool without an adult.

4   All members ____
for permission from a member of staff before using the heaviest weights.

5   Please use a gym towel when exercising. You ____ your own – you can get one at the reception desk.

6   Remember, our staff ____
if you have a health problem. Please don't forget to tell us!

5 Choose the correct words to complete the tips on how to train for a marathon.

The first thing to do is stop delaying and start training! If you **¹**couldn't / can't / aren't able to run very far when you start, don't worry – everyone **²**could / has to / ought start somewhere, and you'll soon get fitter. You **³**must / could / need have a training programme – that's really important. The main idea of your programme is to slowly increase the distance you **⁴**could / are able / can comfortably run, until a marathon doesn't seem such a scary idea. You **⁵**have to / ought / don't need to run every day, but you **⁶**ought / should / are able to try to run at least three times a week. In the last two weeks before the marathon, you **⁷**need / ought to / shouldn't do less, not more. This sounds crazy, but you really **⁸**mustn't / don't have to / ought to get an injury just before the big race – after all your hard work, you want to make sure you enjoy your big day!

PUSH YOURSELF B2

Match the beginnings and ends of the sentences.

1   I've got a splitting ____
2   Lots of people are ill at the moment. I think there's a ____
3   I was in bed all last week, but now I'm back ____
4   I don't feel well. I think I'm coming ____
5   Jill's been really ill, but luckily she's on the ____
6   I feel too ill to go to work today. I think I'll ____
7   I've walked 30 kilometres today, and now my ____
8   I feel really tired today. I think I'm a bit ____

a   call in sick.
b   mend now.
c   bug going around.
d   feet are killing me.
e   on my feet.
f   under the weather.
g   headache. I need to take something for the pain.
h   down with flu.

READING PART 6

For each question, write the correct answer.

Write one word for each gap.

```
● ● ●  ◁ ▷                              🔍 🏠
          To: Laura                      Reply  Forward  ✉
      Subject: Poor you!

   Hi,
   I'm really sorry to hear you broke your leg during the
   half-marathon on Saturday. You poor thing!
   I was so surprised to get your email because you've
   ¹_____ had an accident while running before.
   As you say, at least ²_____ were lots of people
   around you to help. And it was lucky you didn't have
   to wait ³_____ long time for the ambulance to
   arrive to take you to hospital. Did the doctor say how
   long ⁴_____ will be before you can run again?
   Would you like me to ⁵_____ some shopping
   for you, cook you a meal or take you to your hospital
   appointments? Just let me know if I can help
   ⁶_____ all.
   Janie
```

LISTENING

1 09 **Listen to a radio show about fitness apps.**
Which app does Jake suggest for Elly?

- **A** Ten-minute Yoga
- **B** Daily Fit Club
- **C** Burn the Fat
- **D** Superfit in Ten

2 09 **Listen again. Decide if the sentences are true or false.**

1 Elly thinks she is already quite fit.
2 With *Ten-minute Yoga*, you do the same exercises each day.
3 Jake says it's difficult to read the instructions during the workouts with *Ten-minute Yoga*.
4 Jake says the trainer doesn't explain how to do the exercises on *Daily Fit Club*.
5 *Daily Fit Club* is good for people who haven't done much exercise before.
6 Jake says that the workouts on *Burn the Fat* seem very quick.
7 Jake thinks most people would find *Burn the Fat* boring.
8 The first workouts on *Superfit in Ten* are the most difficult.
9 Jake says Elly will only get fitter if she exercises regularly.

SPEAKING

1 Match the beginnings and ends of the phrases for asking about problems, showing sympathy and giving advice.

1	How are	**a**	care.
2	What's	**b**	having a nice hot drink?
3	Take	**c**	wrong?
4	Get	**d**	idea to put ice on an injury like that.
5	You ought	**e**	well soon.
6	Why don't you	**f**	go and see the doctor?
7	How about	**g**	you doing?
8	It's a good	**h**	to stay in bed today.

2 Complete the conversations with words from the box.

feel better	how are	I were you	look after
matter	poor	sorry to hear	why don't you

A: Hi, Amy, ¹ _____ you?

B: Not very well. I think I've got flu.

A: Oh, I hope you ² _____ soon.

A: Hi, George. You look terrible! What's the ³ _____ ?

B: I've got a really bad headache.

A: I'm ⁴ _____ that. If ⁵ _____ , I'd go home and go to bed.

A: Oh, my leg's still really sore from the injury I got on Saturday.

B: ⁶ _____ you! ⁷ _____ go home and rest it?

A: I can't today. I have to go to work. But I'll rest tomorrow.

B: Well, ⁸ _____ yourself!

A: Thanks, I will.

WRITING

1 Add one more letter to correct the spelling mistake in each sentence.

1 I hurt a musle in my leg. _____

2 I've got an apointment to see the doctor. _____

3 Your elbow is in the midle of your arm. _____

4 I've got backace! _____

5 You need your tonge to speak. _____

6 It hurts when I bend my nee. _____

7 I try to eat helthy food. _____

8 My lungs hurt when I breath in. _____

2 Read the email. Correct six mistakes with punctuation, four mistakes with prepositions and two mistakes with modal verbs.

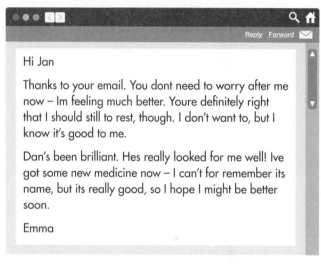

Hi Jan

Thanks to your email. You dont need to worry after me now – Im feeling much better. Youre definitely right that I should still to rest, though. I don't want to, but I know it's good to me.

Dan's been brilliant. Hes really looked for me well! Ive got some new medicine now – I can't for remember its name, but its really good, so I hope I might be better soon.

Emma

Punctuation:
_____
_____
_____
_____

Prepositions:
_____
_____
_____

Modal verbs:
_____
_____

6 ONLINE, OFFLINE

VOCABULARY

1 Read the clues and complete the crossword.

```
  [1]        [2]    [3]   [T]
         [4]              [5]
[6] O     O                [D]
                           
         [7] E      E  [T]
                    
         [8]     [G]
```

Across

2 When you … a photo or piece of writing, you put it online.

6 If you … someone, you see all the updates that they put on Instagram.

7 If you send someone a friend …, you ask them to be a friend online.

8 When you … someone, you add their name to a photo.

Down

1 If you … someone, you stop them seeing photos and things you write.

3 A … is a photo you take of yourself.

4 A … is something you write when a friend has put something online.

5 An … is when you give new information.

2 Choose the correct words to complete the sentences.

1 Carl was being really annoying online, so I *updated / unfriended* him.

2 Hana's just posted a new *story / filter* about her trip to Paris.

3 I don't change my online *status / selfie* very often.

4 Chloe loves using face *comments / filters* – they're really funny!

5 How often do you *update / request* your social media?

6 Ben is worried because he doesn't get many friend *comments / requests*.

3 Read the problem and comments. Complete them with the correct form of the verbs in the box.

break	get	grow	hit	make	rely	turn

LolaB

I'm feeling a bit sad because I **1**_____ up with my boyfriend last month. We gradually **2**_____ apart and in the end we had a big argument and I decided to end the relationship. I don't want to **3**_____ up with him, but I miss him and I can't imagine meeting anyone else. Any ideas?

TomG77

Why don't you **4**_____ to your friends for help? See if they can introduce you to someone new, and you never know – you might **5**_____ it off!

MiaKat

I don't agree with TomG. It isn't fair to **6**_____ on friends to find you a new boyfriend. Why not try a dating app? There's definitely someone out there that you can **7**_____ on well with! Good luck!

GRAMMAR

1 Complete the conversations with the correct form of *will* or *going to* and the verbs in brackets. Think about whether each verb is about a plan, or a decision that someone makes at the time of speaking.

A: Congratulations on your new job in London. When **1**_____ (you / move) there?

B: I'm not sure. I need to find a flat first.

A: Oh, I **2**_____ (help) you look! I love looking at flats!

A: **3**_____ (Harry / come) for a meal with us next weekend?

B: I don't know. I haven't seen him for ages. Maybe I **4**_____ (text) him later to invite him.

A: What's that?

B: It's a book about apps. I **5**_____ (do) a course next year on how to develop new apps.

A: That sounds interesting.

B: I **6**_____ (lend) you the book if you like.

A: Cool.

2 Choose the correct verb forms. Think about whether each verb is about an arrangement or a 'timetable future'.

1 Don't forget we *go / 're going* to the cinema this evening. The film *starts / 's starting* at seven, so don't be late!

2 What *do you do / are you doing* tomorrow evening? Do you want to meet for something to eat?

3 Where are you? You should be here at the station with me. The train *leaves / 's leaving* in 10 minutes!

4 Sorry, I can't come to football training with you this evening. I *meet / 'm meeting* Emma for a drink. ☺

5 Can't chat now. I need to get some food and the supermarket *closes / 's closing* at six.

6 *Do you see / Are you seeing* Paul tomorrow? If so, can you remind him he owes me some money?

3 Complete the predictions with the correct form of *will* or *going to* and the verbs in brackets. Think about whether each one is a general prediction or a prediction where there is a sign that something is going to happen.

1 Oh, no! It's 8.30 already. I .... (miss) my train!

2 I think travel .... (be) more expensive in the future, so people .... (not travel) so much.

3 Look at the sky! I think it .... (rain).

4 We .... (not need) to take a driving test in the future because our cars .... (drive) themselves!

5 Do you think that people .... (ever / live) on Mars?

6 Sam works really hard, so it's obvious that he .... (pass) all his exams.

4 Choose the correct verbs to complete the student's thoughts.

So, college ¹*starts / will start* again today. This year is my final year, so I know it ²*is / 's going to be* difficult. I want to do well, so I ³*'ll work / 'm going to work* really hard, especially at English. I ⁴*'ll meet / 'm meeting* my English teacher this afternoon to talk about things I can do at home to help me improve. I'm sure she ⁵*'ll have / 's having* some good ideas. As part of my plan, I ⁶*'ll stop / 'm going to stop* using social media so much – at the moment I check my phone every few minutes and it really stops me from studying! So I ⁷*don't check / 'm not going to check* my phone until I get home in the evening. But I've just had a message, so I ⁸*'ll start / 'm going to start* that tomorrow!

LISTENING PART 3

 🔊 10 For each question, write the correct answer in the gap.

Write one or two words or a number or a date or a time.

You will hear a journalist called Steffi talking about a week she spent without using social media.

Steffi's Week without Social Media
Steffi started using social media at (**1**) ....
Steffi mainly used social media for posting (**2**) ....
Steffi realised she was spending at least (**3**) .... every day on social media.
When she gave up using social media, Steffi read a (**4**) .... instead.
After one week without social media, Steffi felt less (**5**) ....
Steffi plans to use a (**6**) .... app once a day.

READING

1 Read the article about the future of social media. Choose the best heading for each section A–D. There is one heading you don't need.

1 Bringing the world closer together
2 New ways to use your smartphone
3 The end of the screen
4 New ways to hang out with friends
5 Connected to everything and everyone

What's the future of social media?
Read the opinions of four experts

Twenty-five years ago there was no social media – no Facebook or Instagram, no tweets or sharing of photos. Social media has changed our lives a lot, but where will it be in twenty years' time? We asked four experts.

PUSH YOURSELF /B2

Complete the second sentence so it has a similar meaning to the first. Use the word in brackets.

1 I'm fairly sure that people will travel to Mars one day.
People _____ to Mars one day. (probably)

2 It isn't likely that machines will do all the work for us.
I _____ do all the work for us. (doubt)

3 It's likely that computers will become even smaller.
There's a _____ become even smaller. (chance)

4 I'm sure people won't stop using their phones.
People _____ using their phones. (certainly)

5 It isn't likely that cities will become smaller.
There's _____ cities will become smaller. (chance)

6 I'm 100% certain that people will eat less meat in the future.
People _____ less meat in the future. (definitely)

A _____

All types of technology will use voice controls, so there won't be any more keyboards on our phones. Screens won't be important either, so wanting the latest smartphones with bigger and better screens will be a thing of the past. Instead, we will see holograms – images in the real world, in front of us, and they will look amazingly real. At the moment, we chat with a friend and we look at their face on our phone or computer. In 20 years, we'll be able to see them sitting next to us, looking very much like a real person.
Jacob Stone, Media Director

B _____

I think we will definitely have an electronic device inside our body which will connect us to everything around us. We will be connected to the machines in our homes and places of work, like our cookers and printers. We'll be connected to the internet too, so we'll be able to find information just by thinking about it. And, of course, we'll be connected to each other. I know it sounds a bit crazy at the moment, but I really believe it will be possible to share our thoughts and feelings with each other directly, even when we're in different parts of the world.
Alyssa Tyrone, Creative Manager

C _____

When events happen anywhere in the world, we won't need to send journalists to report on them. There will be hundreds of films, stories and messages from normal people who are there, showing the world what's happening, as it actually happens. People will also be able to share smells and tastes, and even feelings, so it will be possible for everyone to really experience what is happening in another part of the world, whether it's a terrible flood or a fire, a big sporting event or a cultural celebration. We will all feel more connected to each other, and the world will feel a much smaller place.
Amelia Smid, Digital News Editor

D _____

At the moment, I connect with my friends on social media by liking posts, writing comments and uploading photos. In 20 years, I'll disconnect from all this. I'll put on my special glasses and meet my friends in virtual worlds. It will be possible to choose the place, from a beach in Spain to a café in London, and I'll bring together people from my real life and my online friends to have social time together. We'll chat and share jokes, and the experience will feel completely real, even though we'll really all be in different places.
Dev Khan, Digital Product Developer

2 Read the predictions again. Which expert (A–D) thinks ...

1 we won't need a computer or phone to search for something online? _____
2 we won't care so much about the kind of phone we have? _____
3 we will be able to share experiences from all our senses? _____
4 ordinary people will report the news for us? _____
5 we will decide where in the world to see our friends? _____
6 talking to someone on the phone will feel more realistic? _____
7 our real friends and social media friends will meet each other? _____
8 some of the predictions seem difficult to believe right now? _____

SPEAKING

1 Choose the sentence that is NOT relevant as part of an answer to each question.

1 Where do you live?
   A I live in Berlin.
   B I'd like to visit Paris one day.
   C I enjoy living in a big city.

2 What do you do?
   A A lot of people want to work for a bank.
   B It's an interesting job.
   C I work for a bank.

3 How do you get to work or school every day?
   A I sometimes walk if the weather's fine.
   B 300 people work in my office.
   C The buses are usually very busy.

4 Do you think English will be useful for you in the future? Why? / Why not?
   A You need English for a lot of different jobs.
   B I'd like a job where I can travel a lot.
   C I'd like to learn some other languages in the future.

5 What does your family do together?
   A We sometimes go out for meals.
   B Some of my friends don't get on well with their families.
   C I enjoy spending time with my family.

6 Tell us about a teacher that you like.
   A I'm going to leave university next year.
   B His name is Mr Grigson.
   C I always enjoy the lessons.

2 Complete the phrases for gaining time.

1 What do you like doing in your free time?
   Oh, lots of things. _____ see … I really enjoy doing sport, and …

2 Tell us about the place where you live.
   Hmm, _____ where I live. It's a small town in the north of Italy …

3 How much time do you spend on social media?
   _____, to be honest, I don't spend very much time on social media. I …

4 What do you like about your job or school?
   Hmm, _____ about my job. I guess I meet a lot of people and I enjoy that because …

5 Where do you meet your friends?
   OK, _____, I have a lot of friends and we often meet …

6 What do you find difficult about learning English?
   Hmm, _____ difficult. I think probably the most difficult thing for me is …

WRITING

1 Choose the correct words to complete the tips for writing a blog post.

1 It's a *good / bad* idea to show your own personality in what you write.
2 You should *use your own style / copy a successful style*.
3 Try to write *long / short* paragraphs so it doesn't get boring.
4 Use *a formal / an informal* tone.
5 *Ask questions / Make general statements* to help the reader feel involved.
6 *Invite / Don't invite* comments from your readers.

2 Read the sentences from a blog post about friends. Match each sentence that uses a formal tone (1–6) with one that uses an informal tone with a similar meaning (a–f).

1 Everyone understands the importance of friends in our lives. ....
2 There are times when you rely on a friend to give you support. ....
3 Sometimes you can recognise immediately that you will have a long friendship with someone. ....
4 Friends share both good and bad experiences with you. ....
5 Some of your friends may find it difficult to have good relationships with each other. ....
6 When you are experiencing problems, it is clear which of your friends are true friends. ....

a Sometimes you just know that someone will be a friend for life.
b It's hard to imagine life without friends, isn't it?
c When things go wrong, you can see who your real friends are.
d Friends are there for you in good times and bad.
e Sometimes you really need a friend to help you.
f Some of your friends may not hit it off with each other.

3 Choose the two openings that would make you keep reading a blog post about social media.

a Let me start by telling you one of my funniest social media stories.
b Social media is a complete waste of time. I never use social media, but prefer to spend real time with my friends and family.
c This post will discuss the history of social media and its importance in the world today.
d Do you love the way you can connect with people on social media? I certainly do! So, what new forms of social media are coming soon, and how will we use them?

7 WHAT'S YOUR STYLE?

VOCABULARY

1 Complete the conversation with the words in the box.

> afford   fit   look   style   suit   try

A: Oh, look at that dress! I love that long ¹_____,
and the colour would really ²_____ you.
You ³_____ great in blue! Why don't you
⁴_____ it on?

B: It's lovely, but the only size they've got is small, and
I don't think that will ⁵_____ me. Anyway,
I can't ⁶_____ to buy any more clothes!

2 Complete the words in the online adverts.

> A ¹l_____ s_____ white shirt with blue
> ²st_____ p_____ s and a white ³c_____ r.
> There are a few ⁴b_____ t_____ s missing, but
> otherwise it's in perfect condition.
>
> **£3.99**   **BUY IT NOW!**

> Two dresses, both with long ⁵s_____ v_____ s,
> one ⁶p_____ n red, the other blue with a
> flowery ⁷p_____ t_____ n. Only worn once,
> but now too ⁸t_____ g_____ t for me.
>
> **£10 each**   **BUY IT NOW!**

3 Read the clues and complete the puzzle. Then
complete the sentence with the shaded word.

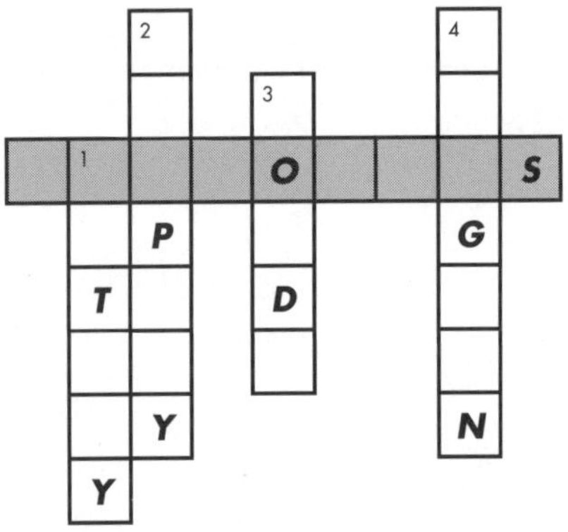

```
        2           4
        
            3
  1     O       S
      P       G
    T       D
      Y       N
    Y
```

1 not neat or tidy
2 an arrangement of things for sale in a shop
3 things that are sold in a shop
4 something that seems cheaper than it should be

This shop likes to keep its _____ happy!

VOCABULARY (right column)

4 Complete the shop review with the correct words.
There are two words you don't need.

> messy   offers   products   reduced
> reductions   sales   shoppers   value

Most ¹_____ will love this shop! Some of the
displays in the shop window look a bit ²_____,
but don't let that put you off. The ³_____ that
they sell are all great, and really good ⁴_____
for money. There are often some great price
⁵_____, and they regularly have special
⁶_____ like two for the price of one.
Definitely worth a visit!

5 Choose the correct words to complete the email.

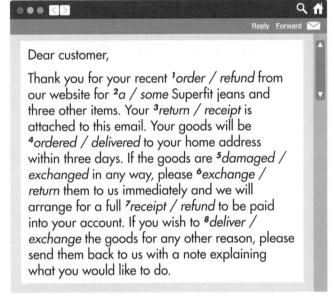

Dear customer,

Thank you for your recent ¹*order / refund* from
our website for ²*a / some* Superfit jeans and
three other items. Your ³*return / receipt* is
attached to this email. Your goods will be
⁴*ordered / delivered* to your home address
within three days. If the goods are ⁵*damaged /
exchanged* in any way, please ⁶*exchange /
return* them to us immediately and we will
arrange for a full ⁷*receipt / refund* to be paid
into your account. If you wish to ⁸*deliver /
exchange* the goods for any other reason, please
send them back to us with a note explaining
what you would like to do.

GRAMMAR

1 Choose the correct verb forms to complete the
reported speech.

1 'I bought my dress online.'
She said that she *bought / had bought / has bought*
her dress online.

2 'I never wear jeans to work!'
He said that he never *wore / had worn / has worn*
jeans to work.

3 'I can't afford to buy a lot of clothes.'
She said that she *can't afford / couldn't afford / won't
afford* to buy a lot of clothes.

4 'I've seen some great bargains in the sales.'
He said that he *saw / 's seen / had seen* some great
bargains in the sales.

2 Complete the reported speech. Remember to change the pronouns as well as the verb tenses.

> We've spent all our money!

1 My friends said that _____ money.

> I'd never been to that shop before.

2 Anna said that _____ that shop before.

> I can help you choose some new trainers.

3 I said to Dan that _____ some new trainers.

> I'll lend you my jacket.

4 I told Maria that _____ jacket.

> I love your new shirt.

5 Mia told me that _____ new shirt.

> I must get some new trainers!

6 Paul said that _____ new trainers.

3 Choose *say* or *tell*.

1 Al *said / told* me that he doesn't wear ties.
2 Carl *said / told* that the department store had some great bargains.
3 She didn't want to *say / tell* me how much she had paid for her boots.
4 The shop assistant *said / told* to me that this style was very popular.
5 Charlie *said / told* me all about her trip to London.
6 I asked her if the prices would be reduced, but she *said / told* no.

4 Read the questions and answers. Then complete the reported speech.

1

Paul: Where are you going?
Me: I'm going to the department store.
Paul asked me _____ .
I told _____ to the department store.

2

Anna: Do you like my new dress?
Me: It looks amazing!
Anna asked me _____ new dress.
I said _____ amazing.

3

Maria: When will you start your new job?
John: I'm not sure.
Maria asked John _____ new job.
John said _____ sure.

4

My sister: Did you find any bargains?
Me: I found a few.
My sister asked me _____ any bargains.
I told _____ a few.

5

Eva: What have you bought?
Me: I've bought some new shoes.
Eva asked me _____ .
I said _____ some new shoes.

6

Carlo: Are you going to ask for a refund?
Lisa: I've already done it.
Carlo asked Lisa _____ a refund.
Lisa said _____ it.

LISTENING

1 11 **Listen to the first part of a podcast about clothes. What are *ethical* clothes?**

A expensive clothes that are fashionable and look good
B clothes that are made in a way that doesn't harm the environment or people
C clothes that are cheap, so people can afford them

2 12 **Listen to the rest of the podcast. Choose the sentence that sums up the ideas.**

A Ethical clothes are good for the planet and people, and they also look good.
B Ethical clothes help animals and they are often cheaper than other clothes.
C Ethical clothes sound like a good idea, but they don't really exist.

3 12 **Listen again. Answer the questions.**

1 What is unusual about the trainers Kiera talks about?
2 What does this company no longer use in its stores?
3 What happens to most clothes when they go into the ground as rubbish?
4 What is different about the Swedish company's clothes?
5 What can people do if they can't afford to buy the Swedish company's clothes?
6 Why are some clothes on GoodClothes.com suitable for vegetarians?
7 Why does Kiera think she won't buy a T-shirt from GoodClothes.com?

Read the conversation between Milly and a shop assistant, then complete what Milly says about the conversation. For each sentence, choose one of the verbs in brackets.

Milly: OK. I'll take this bag, please.

Assistant: Lovely. Can you come to the till, please?

Milly: Of course. Is it possible to clean the bag if it gets dirty?

Assistant: Yes. If you need to clean it, you should use a special cleaner. We've got some here, for £6.00.

Milly: Right. I'll take that, too.

Assistant: OK. Now, it's important that you don't get this bag wet, otherwise the colour might come out.

Milly: OK. It's a present for a friend, Sara. Is it possible for her to exchange it, if she doesn't like it?

Assistant: Of course. Keep the receipt, and if she brings it back with the receipt we'll definitely exchange it for her.

Milly: Thanks.

Assistant: There you are. And would you like to come to our special sales evening? There will be some great price reductions.

Milly: Oh, yes please.

1 The shop assistant _____asked me to come_____ to the till. (warn / ask / promise)

2 She _____ a special cleaner on the bag. (invite / promise / advise)

3 She _____ the bag wet. (ask / warn / promise)

4 She _____ the bag if Sara doesn't like it. (invite / ask / promise)

5 She _____ the receipt. (tell / invite / warn)

6 She _____ come to a special sales evening. (promise / advise / invite)

For each question, choose the correct answer.

1
> These headphones can only be returned for a refund if the plastic box is unopened and in perfect condition.

A You won't be able to get your money back if you've damaged the box.

B If you don't like these headphones after using them, return them for a refund.

C These headphones are in the sale because the plastic box they're in is damaged.

2
> Wash at 30 degrees by hand or in machine, using any cleaning liquid suitable for silk. Always wash separately and dry flat.

A After washing this shirt by hand, hang it up to dry.

B Avoid washing this shirt together with other clothes.

C Any cleaning product may be used to wash this shirt.

3
> **Welcome to Unique Fashions** – the newest store on the web! Click here for a free gift in exchange for signing up to our weekly email.

A Unique Fashions are offering rewards to everyone placing their first web order.

B Customers who order online from Unique Fashions this week will receive a reward.

C There is a reward for anyone who agrees to receive emails from Unique Fashions.

4
> Daisy,
> I went to the 50% off sale at Greens Department Store. The jeans you bought were all gone but I got some fantastic bargains in the sports department, including a pair of trainers.
> Morgan

A Morgan found fewer bargains in the department store sale than Daisy did.

B Morgan bought something different to her friend Daisy in the sale.

C Morgan managed to buy some trainers at less than half the original price.

5
> ## Need a different size?
> Our changing room staff will be pleased to fetch this for you. Just ask.

A If you find something is too tight, changing room staff can bring a bigger size.

B Our changing room staff are happy to check for you what size you are.

C Please give anything that's the wrong size to changing room staff when you leave.

SPEAKING

1 Choose the correct words to complete the responses.

1 **A:** I'd love to go shopping in New York.
  B: So *would / do* I.

2 **A:** I often get new clothes for my birthday.
  B: *Also / Same* here.

3 **A:** I don't often buy things from department stores.
  B: Me *also / neither*.

4 **A:** I think it's much easier to shop online.
  B: I know what you *say / mean*.

5 **A:** I love it when the shops are really busy in the sales.
  B: *Would / Do* you? I hate it!

6 **A:** I always try shoes on before I buy them.
  B: I do *too / also*.

2 Choose the best response.

1 I don't like those trainers.
  A So do I.
  B Do you?
  C Neither do I.

2 I love bright colours!
  A That's a good point.
  B Same here.
  C So am I.

3 Sometimes it's difficult to find something that fits you.
  A Me too.
  B Do you?
  C I know what you mean.

4 I always get excited when the sales start.
  A So do I.
  B Me neither.
  C So am I.

5 A lot of clothes are cheaper online.
  A Me too.
  B That's a good point.
  C So do I.

6 I'd like to work for a fashion company.
  A Me neither.
  B I am too.
  C So would I.

WRITING

1 Match the beginnings and ends of these sentences for a review.

1 There's a very good selection ....
2 The best thing about ....
3 The only thing that's not good ....
4 It's definitely worth ....
5 I'd certainly ....
6 What I like ....
7 My only ....

a is the delivery time.
b recommend this site.
c of products.
d most about this site is how easy it is to use.
e this website is the prices.
f complaint is that the colours are too pale.
g checking out this site.

2 Decide if the sentences are positive or negative. Write P or N.

1 Their products are amazing quality. ....
2 The range is extremely limited. ....
3 Some of their things are not the best value. ....
4 There's an incredible variety of goods. ....
5 The prices are very reasonable. ....
6 They're rather expensive. ....

3 Choose the correct linking words.

1 *Although / But* the quality is good, the range is fairly limited.

2 The staff are extremely helpful *and / though* they certainly know all about the products.

3 There's a great variety of products. The prices are extremely high, *as well / though*.

4 The staff are really friendly, *but / and* they're often too busy to help you.

5 Most of their products are good quality, and the prices are very reasonable *as well / though*.

4 Complete the review with the words and phrases in the box. There are three you don't need.

> as well   but   complaint   selection   like most
> not so good   reasonable   recommend
> the best thing   worth

This is an amazing online shoe shop! There's a great
¹ _____ of shoes and boots, and the prices
are very ² _____. What I ³ _____
about this website is the fact that they give extra
information like 'these shoes are best for people with
narrow feet.' My only ⁴ _____ is that the shoes
took a week to arrive, ⁵ _____ I'm really
pleased with them. It's definitely ⁶ _____
checking out this site, and I would certainly
⁷ _____ their shoes!

8 INTO THE WILD

VOCABULARY

1 Read the clues and complete the puzzle. Then put the shaded letters in order to answer the question.

```
¹C   |   | V |   |
² | H | O |   |   |
³ |   | V |   | S |
⁴C |   |   | F |
⁵S |   | N |   | S |
⁶ |   | E |   | V |   | S |
⁷ |   |   | V |   | B |   | K |
```

1   It might be fun to explore inside here, but it's very dark.
2   I love walking along this, next to the sea.
3   If there's a storm at sea, these are very big.
4   I like climbing up this and then looking down at the sea below.
5   These can be big or small, and you find them on the ground.
6   All trees have these, and they're usually green.
7   You can sometimes walk along here, next to the river.
8   Where would Katy love to go? _____

2 Unjumble the letters to complete the sentences.

1   There were colourful birds on the _____ of the trees. (bnareshc)
2   It was fun walking across the _____ _____ in the desert. (dans dnesu)
3   You can't sail your boat over the _____! (weratafll)
4   There are no trees here, but there are lots of small _____. (shubes)
5   If you climb a high mountain, you may have to climb over a _____. (galcrie)
6   The ship sank when it hit an _____. (ciebreg)

3 Read what the people say about the places. Choose the correct adjective for each place.

1   There are no sounds here at all!   *humid / quiet*
2   There are so many bushes, we can't get through!   *dense / dry*
3   There's nothing in this cave!   *noisy / empty*
4   There's very little rain here.   *dry / dense*
5   There are so many birds here, and they're all singing!   *quiet / noisy*
6   It's hot here, and the air feels wet.   *empty / humid*

4 Complete the names of four habitats. Then match each one to a definition.

1   g ____ s ____ l ____ d s
2   t ____ p ____ l f ____ t s
3   t ____ m ____ r ____ e f ____ t s
4   p ____ l r r ____ g ____ s

A   It's very cold here for most of the year, and there's a lot of snow.
B   There are very few trees or bushes here, but plenty of space for animals to move around.
C   The trees and bushes are very dense, and it's also hot and humid.
D   There are lots of trees here, and the weather is never too hot or too cold.

5 Read the clues and complete the animal names.

1   I'm a bird, but I can't fly. p ____ n
2   I've got big back legs and I move around by jumping. k ____ o
3   I'm small and brown, and I've got thin, sharp parts all over my body to protect me. h ____ g
4   I use my long neck to reach up and eat leaves on the trees. g ____ e
5   I'm a big, strong animal with thick, white fur and I live at the North Pole. p ____ r b ____ r
6   I'm small, I live in trees and I've got a thick tail. r ____ d s ____ l
7   I look like a big monkey, and I've got red fur. o ____ gu ____ n
8   I eat grass and live in large groups. I can run fast to escape from animals that hunt me. r ____ d d ____ r
9   I live in very cold areas, and you can often hear me calling at night. a ____ c w ____ f
10   I'm quite big and brightly coloured, and I've got hard skin, with no fur. g ____ n i ____ a

6 Complete the advert with the correct *-ed* or *-ing* adjectives based on the verbs.

RAINFOREST ADVENTURE!

Do you want a ¹ _____ (challenge) holiday this year? Why not come on a rainforest adventure! You definitely won't be ² _____ (disappoint)! You'll see some ³ _____ (amaze) animals, and experience one of the most ⁴ _____ (excite) places on Earth! You don't need to feel ⁵ _____ (worry) about dangers, because the trip is carefully planned with safety in mind, and it ends with a ⁶ _____ (relax) few days in a luxury hotel. Visit our website today for more details – you'll be ⁷ _____ (surprise) how low our prices are!

GRAMMAR

1 Choose the correct modals of speculation to complete the email.

🔍 🏠
Reply Forward ✉

Hi Jo,

This is day five of my jungle adventure, and we're staying in a small hotel tonight – luxury! It's really hot, and there are dark clouds, so I think it ¹*could / must* rain again soon. We can hear lots of monkeys in the jungle, but our guide says we ²*couldn't / may not* see them because they stay high up in the trees. There are also lots of snakes, and I'm sure some of them ³*can / must* be poisonous, which is a bit scary. We keep seeing things moving in the river. Freddie says they ⁴*can't / mustn't* be crocodiles because there aren't any in this region, but I still think I ⁵*can / may* stay well away from the water! It ⁶*can / might* be a while before I can write again because we're going deeper into the jungle, and I'm sure there ⁷*can't / must* be wi-fi there!

Take care,

Mia

---

2 Complete the second sentence so it has a similar meaning to the first. Choose the correct modal in brackets to give the correct meaning.

1 I'm sure Dan isn't scared of spiders!
Dan _____ of spiders!
(might / can't / must)

2 It's possible that I will go to Africa next summer.
I _____ to Africa next summer.
(may / can / must)

3 It's possible that we won't see any lions.
We _____ any lions.
(might not / couldn't / can't)

4 Maybe there are sharks in the water.
There _____ sharks in the water.
(can / could / must)

5 It's possible that there aren't any tigers here.
There _____ any tigers here.
(can't / may not / couldn't)

6 I'm sure it's difficult living in the Arctic Circle.
It _____ living in the Arctic Circle. (can / could / must)

PUSH YOURSELF /B2

Complete the animal fact file with the correct words.

ANIMAL FACTS

1 Most kinds of deer have short t ___ i ___ s. The males use their a ___ t ___ rs for fighting.

2 Elephants can lift almost 350 kilos with their t ___ n ___ s. Unfortunately, they are often killed for their t ___ ks.

3 Some horses have long m ___ n ___ s which can grow down to their knees. Horses are not the only animals that have h ___ v ___ s – sheep, deer, camels and giraffes also have them.

4 Tigers' feet have soft p ___ s but very sharp c ___ ws, which can grow to over 10 cm long!

5 The Australian pelican is a large bird with black and white f ___ th ___ s. It has a very large b ___ k which it uses for catching fish and which can be from 30 to 50 cm long!

1 Read the article about wild swimming. Match the headings with the paragraphs. There is one heading you don't need.

1. Wild swimming in the city
2. What is wild swimming?
3. Bored with the swimming pool?
4. Why is it popular?
5. Is it safe?

2 Read the article again. Decide if the sentences are true or false.

1. Wild swimming is becoming more popular.
2. Wild swimmers accept that water in rivers and lakes isn't as clean as the water in swimming pools.
3. Most wild swimmers want to enjoy an extreme experience.
4. The main danger in rivers and lakes is from fast-moving water.
5. People can find safety advice about wild swimming online.
6. People have always swum in the canals in Paris.

A

There's nothing like the feeling of diving into cool water on a hot summer's day! But for some, the traditional swimming pool just isn't exciting enough. Instead, they are looking for something more challenging, and are turning to wild swimming in increasing numbers.

B

Wild swimming simply means swimming in a natural environment, like the sea, a river or a lake. Fans of the sport say that it is a great way to feel connected with the natural world. They also argue that, although pollution exists, natural water is generally cleaner than that in swimming pools because nothing is added to it, and it isn't full of crowds of people. For the few who are more adventurous, there is the extra challenge of finding more extreme places to test the water, like icy mountain lakes!

C

It must be exciting to swim in such places, but there are dangers, too, and anyone thinking of trying wild swimming should think carefully about safety. Many lakes and rivers are very deep. The water may be fast-moving, and it can be difficult to swim against this movement. But even more worrying than this, there could be hidden plants or rubbish under the surface. For this reason, it's a good idea to always walk into the water rather than diving in head first. To help people avoid the dangers, there are several websites which offer advice on safe places to swim.

D

But fortunately, it isn't only in the countryside that people can enjoy a wild swim. Many big cities have rivers and canals running through their centres, and some are now opening these to swimmers. In Paris, for example, people can now swim in one of the main canals in the city. Swimming wasn't allowed in the canal for nearly a hundred years because of pollution, but in 2017 the government declared that the water was safe and announced official swimming areas with safety officers to make sure there were no accidents. The swimmers soon took advantage of this in their thousands, as it perhaps offers the perfect solution of a wild swimming experience in a safe environment!

LISTENING PART 4

🔊 13 **For each question, choose the correct answer.**

You will hear an interview with a man called Rob Tucker, who is an expert on Australian camels.

1 Rob became interested in camels when he
   A read a book about a journey.
   B got a holiday job on a sheep farm.
   C saw a documentary film about camels.

2 Rob says that camels brought to Australia in the 1860s
   A were mainly from Arabian countries.
   B were stronger than camels born in Australia.
   C were accompanied by people who could ride them.

3 Why does Rob think camels were more useful than horses in Australia?
   A They could go for days without drinking water.
   B They could travel over difficult ground.
   C They could walk all day without needing breaks.

4 Why do some Australian farmers today complain about the camels?
   A They damage houses.
   B They break water pipes.
   C They eat the farm animals' food.

5 Rob recommends a camel ride that lasts
   A half a day.
   B one day.
   C three days.

6 Rob says it's sometimes hard to see camels in the wild because
   A they stay away from the roads.
   B their colour is similar to the landscape.
   C the camel population has recently decreased.

SPEAKING

Look at the photo and complete the sentences for describing it with the correct words.

background	can see	middle	might
must be	on	sure	there's	this is

1 .... a picture of a sports adventure.
2 .... a small beach, which is empty.
3 The sea is .... the right.
4 In the .... of the picture we .... a man.
5 He's running along the shore, and it .... quite cold because he's wearing long trousers and a sweatshirt.
6 There's a small object on the grass. I'm not .... what it is.
7 The man is carrying a rucksack. I guess it .... be to carry some food and drink.
8 In the ...., there are some tall cliffs.

WRITING

1 **Choose the adjective which does NOT fit in each sentence.**

1 There's a small restaurant near the beach which serves *fresh / relaxing / delicious* food.
2 You can walk along the *high / rocky / clear* cliffs.
3 It's lovely to swim in the lovely *long / cool / clear* water.
4 There are *amazing / high / fantastic* views from the top of the mountain.
5 There are also some very *fresh / interesting / exciting* towns to visit.
6 It's a great place to come for a *relaxing / rocky / long* holiday.

2 **Choose the correct linking words.**

1 Corsica is an island in the Mediterranean *and / but* it's a great place to visit.
2 *Although / But* it's quite small, there are lots of things to do.
3 Corsica is a part of France, *because / so* people speak French there.
4 There are plenty of beautiful beaches *as well as / also* mountains where you can go walking.
5 I love Corsica *because / so* it's so quiet and peaceful.
6 *What's more / Although,* there are lots of hotels which aren't too expensive.

9 ALWAYS LEARNING

VOCABULARY

1 Complete what the student says about school. Use the highlighted letters to complete the final sentence.

> It's really important to ¹a _ _ _ t _ _ d school. ²E _ _ c _ _ _ _ _ _ n is important, and it's difficult to get a good job if you don't have ³q _ _ l _ _ c _ _ _ _ _ _ s. I try to work hard for exams and I usually get good ⁴g _ _ d _ s. We also learn a lot of useful ⁵ _ k _ _ l _ at school, like planning tasks and working together. The only thing I don't like about school is all the ⁶ _ _ _ _ _ _ _ _ !

2 Complete each sentence with two of the words given.

1   What's the _____ of tomorrow's _____? I hope it's interesting!
    (degree / lecture / topic)
2   Did you _____ all your exams last _____? I hope you did!
    (pass / term / tutor)
3   I can't believe that I'll _____ and get my _____ this summer!
    (degree / fail / graduate)
4   It's simple – if you don't _____ enough, you'll _____ your exams!
    (fail / revise / pass)

3 Choose the correct words to complete the tips.

HOW TO BE A TOP STUDENT

1   It's important to listen carefully in lectures. This will help you to *take / do* good notes.

2   Always *do / make* homework on time, so you're ready for the next piece of work.

3   *Pay / Give* attention when tutors or other people are talking to you.

4   Try to *do / make* extra research on your own, outside class.

5   If you *do / make* a mistake, learn from it!

6   Make sure you get enough sleep before you *make / take* an exam.

7   Be proud of yourself when you finally *get / make* your degree – it's a great achievement!

GRAMMAR

1 Choose the correct words to complete the passive sentences.

1   All students *is / are* expected to work hard.
2   Our maths class *is / was* cancelled yesterday.
3   We *was / were* told our exam results yesterday.
4   Lunch *is / are* served between 12.30 and 1.30.
5   I think that students now *are / were* given too much homework.
6   Spanish *doesn't / isn't* taught in all schools in the UK.

2 Complete the passive sentences.

1   Paul and Mel's parents sent them to a private school.
    Paul and Mel _____ to a private school.
2   A famous actor opened the show.
    The show _____ a famous actor.
3   The school spends a lot of money on new books.
    A lot of money _____ on new books.
4   They don't sell crisps in the school shop now.
    Crisps _____ in the school shop now.
5   The teacher didn't tell us about the school trip.
    We _____ about the school trip.
6   A problem with the electrical system caused the fire.
    The fire _____ a problem with the electrical system.

3 Complete the conversations with the passive form of the verbs in the box.

encourage	not include	not invite
send	steal	tell

A: Is this a good college?
B: Yes. The teachers are good, and everyone ¹ _____ to work hard.

A: Where's your bike?
B: It ² _____ yesterday! I'm so annoyed!

A: How do you usually get your exam results?
B: They ³ _____ by email, or you can look on the college website.

A: Have we got an exam tomorrow?
B: Yes! We ⁴ _____ about it last week!

A: I was surprised that Dan wasn't at the party on Saturday.
B: Me too. He ⁵ _____ for some reason.

A: £50 seems cheap for the school trip to London.
B: Yes, but remember food ⁶ _____ in that price.

For each question, choose the correct answer.

Teacher Jack Greening talks about setting up a school photography club

Last year the headteacher came and asked me to start a photography club. Our school already has lots of fantastic sports clubs, which is great, but not all students like sport. My classroom's decorated with photos I've taken, but they're not exactly works of art and I wasn't sure I was a good enough photographer to teach others. But I wanted to run a school club and the headteacher promised money for cameras, memory cards, tripods, and so on – so I said yes.

There were so many things to consider before I started, and I knew my colleagues were too busy to help. Should the club be for students with experience? Should it be for the whole school, or only some year-groups? Above all, what did I want to achieve? To enter student competitions, or just to take photos for the school website? In the end I decided my aim was for beginners to have fun with photography. I held the sessions in a science lab where we could lock stuff that we needed for the club in a cupboard.

About fifteen students came to the first session. Some of them were clearly only there to be with their mates. Still, I got them all to take photos of each other. We put these on the screen and the keen students chatted about the good and not so good points. I hadn't expected them to have so many good ideas about what they could do better next time.

The second week, most of the students came back, and another twenty-five joined. I had to ask the headteacher to get another teacher to share the sessions. Colleagues heard students talking about the club in lessons and advised me about things to do with students, including taking them to a famous photographer's exhibition. A year later, and I've no regrets about starting this club. The students have worked hard on their photography. Some clearly have a natural ability, which helps. I've already planned next year's photographic projects, but our school cameras are quite basic. To take really amazing photos, the students need a more advanced one of their own – that's the best way to improve.

1 How did Jack feel when he was first asked to set up the photography club?
- **A** stressed because he had enough to do already
- **B** worried by the lack of photography equipment
- **C** anxious about his photography skills
- **D** disappointed as he wanted to run a sports club

2 In the second paragraph, what does Jack say was the most important thing for him to decide?
- **A** how much help he would need
- **B** which students the club was for
- **C** where sessions would take place
- **D** what the purpose of the club was

3 What surprised Jack at the club's first session?
- **A** how many different types of students took part
- **B** how good most of the students' photos were
- **C** how well students could discuss their photos
- **D** how serious all the students were about photography

4 How did Jack's colleagues react when they heard about his club?
- **A** They suggested some possible activities.
- **B** They offered to run the sessions with Jack.
- **C** They asked Jack for advice about their own clubs.
- **D** They recommended some students to join the club.

5 What might Jack say to the parents of students in his photography club?
- **A** 'I've enjoyed helping your children this year, but in order to make further progress they now need to do a proper photography course.'
- **B** 'Some of your children had the advantage of previous experience using cameras, but they've all made great progress.'
- **C** 'If your children are interested in becoming better photographers, encourage them by taking them to see photography exhibitions.'
- **D** 'To be a great photographer requires talent and lots of practice, but it helps if your children have good cameras too.'

Complete the passive sentences.

1   Someone has broken a window in one of the classrooms.
    A window in one of the classrooms _____
    _____ .

2   Someone is repairing the school minibus at the moment.
    The school minibus _____
    at the moment.

3   They had announced the winner two weeks earlier.
    The winner _____
    two weeks earlier.

4   They should clean the classrooms every day.
    The classrooms _____
    every day.

5   Everyone must complete their project by Friday.
    All projects _____
    by Friday.

6   You can't use dictionaries in the exam.
    Dictionaries _____
    in the exam.

LISTENING

1 **14 Listen to a radio discussion about learning. Which sentence best summarises the discussion?**

A   Stella Bradshaw talks about her own experiences of learning different skills through her life.

B   Stella Bradshaw discusses which new skills are the best ones to learn as an adult.

C   Stella Bradshaw talks about the advantages of continuing to learn new things as an adult.

2 **14 Listen again. Decide if the sentences are true or false.**

1   Stella wrote her book because of her own experiences.

2   Mavis Bowman left school because she wasn't keen on learning when she was a teenager.

3   According to Stella, older people don't learn as quickly as younger people.

4   Stella says the main reason for learning new things as an adult is that it makes life more interesting.

5   Kevin learned to ride a bike quite easily when he was 28.

6   Stella's advice to listeners is to avoid things that they found very difficult when they were younger.

SPEAKING

1 Match the sentence halves about people's likes and dislikes at school.

1 I love ....

2 I'm not very interested ....

3 When I was younger, I was quite good ....

4 I'm bored ....

5 I can't ....

6 I'm quite keen ....

a at maths.

b stand economics!

c chemistry and biology.

d on English.

e by physics.

f in history.

2 Complete what the people say with one word in each gap.

1 I .... mind biology, but I hate physics!

2 I've always been terrible .... art.

3 I really don't like history. I .... it really dull!

4 I'm fascinated .... different countries, so I love geography.

5 I .... bear IT – it's my worst subject!

6 When I was younger, I .... maths was boring, but now I know how important it is.

WRITING

1 Complete the email with the words in the box.

could	dear	enquire	finally
know	let	look	sincerely

---

1 .... Mr Green,

I am writing to ² .... about the drama course at Homewood Hall.
Please ³ .... you tell me how long the course lasts? I would also like to ⁴ .... if all the equipment is provided.
⁵ ...., please could you ⁶ .... me know if there are still vacancies on the course?
I ⁷ .... forward to hearing from you.

Yours ⁸ ....,

Emma Ashton

2 Complete the indirect questions. Use the word in brackets.

1 Where does the course take place?
I'd ....
.... place. (know)

2 Is food included in the price?
Please could ....
.... the price. (tell)

3 What should I bring with me?
Please ....
.... bring with me. (let)

4 Can I get to the college by bus?
Please could ....
.... the college by bus. (tell)

5 Is there a minimum age for students?
I'd ....
.... a minimum age for students. (know)

6 Is the course fully booked?
Please ....
.... fully booked. (let)

VOCABULARY

1 Read the clues and complete the puzzle. Then write the mystery word in the shaded column.

1 the place where boats arrive and leave from
2 a large boat that carries passengers and sometimes cars
3 a situation when the cars and lorries on the road cannot move forwards (2 words)
4 a journey by plane
5 the place where a train leaves from at a railway station
6 a situation when a train, bus or plane is late
7 a place where you can buy fuel for your car (2 words)

Mystery word: ....
Clue: It's important, so don't lose it! (2 words)

Crossword:
- Vertical (shaded): P A N S
- 1 P _ _
- 2 F _
- 3 T _ _ _ _ _ J _
- 4 F _ _
- 5 P _ _ _ F _ M
- 6 D _ _
- 7 P _ _ _ _ _ T

2 Complete the advice about flying with the words in the box.

airline	business class	cabin staff	check-in
cockpit	departure lounge	flight attendant	gate

TIPS FOR STRESS-FREE FLYING

1 When you buy your ticket, think about paying a bit more for a .... seat – they're a lot more comfortable!

2 Make sure you know which .... you are travelling with before you get to the airport.

3 When you get to the airport, go straight to .... to collect your boarding pass.

4 Wait in the .... until your plane is ready to board.

5 When your plane is ready to board, go to the correct ....

6 The .... will greet you as you get on the plane.

7 If you have any problems during your flight, speak to a ....

8 Remember, it is against the law to try to enter the .... where the pilot is sitting!

3 Complete the comments about travel experiences opposite with the correct form of a phrasal verb. Use *get* and the correct particle from the box.

around	back	into	off	out of	to

What's your best, worst or funniest travel experience?

We'd love to know!

JennaJ
Last year, my friend and I ¹.............................. a tuk tuk taxi in India to take us up a steep hill. But the taxi was so old, it couldn't get up the hill! In the end, we ².............................. the taxi and walked! 😄

Sam88
I once chose to visit a small village in Italy because there was a train station there and I liked the name. But when I ³.............................. the train, I found there was nothing there except a few houses – and no more trains until the next day!

LucyLu
My cousin and I were visiting the Greek islands last summer and hired bikes to ⁴.............................. . Unfortunately, I fell off and ended up in hospital!

James123
I once decided to walk from the airport to my hotel, to save money. It took me five hours, and I was exhausted when I finally ⁵.............................. my hotel!

TomG
I was on a flight into London last year, but there was a storm so they took us to Hamburg. I finally ⁶.............................. home 26 hours later!

GRAMMAR

1 Complete the zero conditional sentences with the correct form of the verbs in brackets. There is one verb in each group that you don't need.

1 When I _____ on holiday, I _____ to travel by plane. (prefer / go / arrive)

2 Everyone _____ if the train _____ late. (be / complain / get)

3 I always _____ better when I _____ to work. (walk / like / feel)

4 You _____ a lot of money if you _____ your bike to get around the city. (use / get / save)

5 If you _____ your tickets in advance, they _____ much cheaper. (be / cost / buy)

2 Complete the dialogues with the correct form of the verbs to make first conditional sentences.

1 **A:** Shall we walk to the cinema?
   B: No – it's raining! We _____ (get) wet if we _____ (walk)!

2 **A:** What _____ (we / do) if Jack _____ (not / be) at the airport to meet us?
   B: We'll call him – I've got his number.

3 **A:** Is it time to go?
   B: Yes, and you need to hurry up. You _____ (miss) your plane unless you _____ (leave) now!

4 **A:** I'll pay for the coffees.
   B: Thanks. If you _____ (pay) for these, I _____ (buy) you a sandwich on the flight!

5 **A:** Are you going to get the train to Oxford tomorrow?
   B: No, I _____ (go) by car, unless the roads _____ (be) too busy.

3 Complete the second sentence so it has a similar meaning to the first. Use the word in brackets.

1 We'll only go to the beach if it's sunny.
   We won't _____ sunny. (unless)

2 We'll go to the concert unless the tickets are too expensive.
   We _____ too expensive. (won't)

3 If I pass all my exams, my parents will buy me a car.
   My parents _____ I pass all my exams. (unless)

4 We won't get a taxi unless there are no buses.
   We'll _____ buses. (only)

5 I'll buy some shoes if I see some that I like.
   I won't _____ some that I like. (any)

6 I'll come to the party unless I have a lot of homework.
   I _____ a lot of homework. (if)

4 Complete the sentences with the zero or first conditional form of the verb in brackets.

1 I always _____ (walk) through the park when it _____ (is) sunny.

2 I _____ (call) you from the station later if there _____ (be) any delays with the trains.

3 If I _____ (see) Rob this afternoon, I _____ (tell) him you're looking for him.

4 Tara always _____ (get) annoyed if the bus _____ (be) late!

5 If I _____ (go) to work early, there _____ (be) always plenty of seats on the train.

6 What _____ (you / do) if your car _____ (break down) on the motorway tomorrow?

5 Complete the text with the correct second conditional form of the verbs.

SHOULD WE SIMPLY STOP USING PLASTIC?

A lot of people think the world *1* _____ (be) a better place if we *2* _____ (stop) using plastic. But is it really that simple? For example, if we *3* _____ (use) glass bottles for things like milk, they *4* _____ (be) heavier. If lorries *5* _____ (have to) carry more weight, they *6* _____ (use) more fuel, and this *7* _____ (cause) more pollution. Also, if we *8* _____ (not / have) plastic for things like bags and phone cases, companies *9* _____ (make) more things out of leather, so we *10* _____ (have) more animals, and they *11* _____ (need) more water and food. A lot of clothes use plastic too, and if we *12* _____ (change) to more natural materials, we *13* _____ (grow) more cotton, which *14* _____ (use) a lot of natural resources. As you can see, the *problem* of plastic is simple, but the solutions are much more difficult!

6 Complete the sentences with the correct form of the verbs in brackets.

1 If I _____ (have) lots of money, I would travel all around the world!

2 Our old car never starts easily when the weather _____ (be) cold.

3 I'll go for a pizza with you on Saturday if I _____ (have) enough money.

4 If I _____ (eat) chocolate, it gives me a headache.

5 If the trains were more comfortable, more people _____ (use) them.

6 If you tell me what time your train arrives tomorrow, I _____ (come) to the station to meet you.

7 I'll ride my bike to college tomorrow unless I _____ (have) a lot of books to carry.

8 You would be much fitter if you _____ (walk) to work every day!

READING

1 **Read the article. Which sentence best sums up what the article says?**

A Plastic rubbish on beaches isn't a big problem yet, but it will be in a few years.

B Plastic rubbish on beaches is a big problem, but people are finding creative solutions.

C The problem of plastic rubbish on beaches is getting worse, and the government should do something about it.

A SEA OF PLASTIC

A recent storm in the south west of England brought an unexpected problem – large amounts of plastic rubbish on the beaches. The oceans are full of plastic, and when a storm moves the water more than usual, it can also lift this rubbish from the bottom of the sea and move it to the shore. It is clearly a big problem, but some people are now taking action themselves:

The power of volunteers

In one town, a group of local people have decided to clean up their beach themselves. Although they are all volunteers, so they aren't paid, they spend every weekend down on the shore, collecting as much rubbish as they can. They put it into different bags, depending on the type. They sell anything valuable, recycle as much as possible, and leave the rest to be taken away as rubbish. They also encourage tourists who use the beach to pick up five pieces of rubbish before they leave.

From rubbish to art

One family is using art to make people think about the problem of plastic in the oceans. Sara and John Bailey, together with their two children, regularly collect rubbish from the beach near their home and use it to create works of art. Sara says they have great fun together choosing which things to use and thinking of clever ways to use them. The works of art go into local shops, and the money they make from them pays for any materials that they need.

Boats to collect more rubbish

A bigger project is using plastic from the oceans to create useful products for local people. The project, which receives financial help from the government, collects plastic from the beach. It sends it to a local factory, where it is recycled and made into kayaks, or small boats. These kayaks go back to local people at no cost, and people can then use them to spend time on the sea collecting more plastic.

Although governments clearly need to take action to deal with the problem of plastic in the oceans, it seems that individuals and local groups can also be a big part of the solution.

2 **Read the article again. Which project are the sentences about? Write V (volunteer plastic pickers), A (the art project) or K (the kayak project).**

1 They sort the rubbish that they collect. ....

2 They give the things that they make to local people. ....

3 The project receives money to pay for the work. ....

4 They enjoy the work that they do. ....

5 They try to persuade other people to join in and help. ....

6 They sell the things that they make. ....

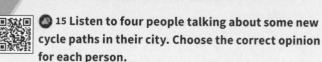

PUSH YOURSELF B2

🔊 **15 Listen to four people talking about some new cycle paths in their city. Choose the correct opinion for each person.**

1 **A** They're good, but they're quite dangerous.

B They're good, and safe to use at any time.

C They're only useful during the day.

2 **A** They're not very good, and the signs aren't easy to see.

B They're excellent, and you can easily see where you're going.

C They're quite good, but difficult to follow.

3 **A** They aren't good at all.

B They're quite good, but there should be more of them.

C They're very good, and they should advertise them more.

4 **A** They're not useful because there aren't enough of them.

B They're useful, but they're sometimes too crowded.

C They're very useful, especially in the mornings.

LISTENING PART 2

🔊 16 **For each question, choose the correct answer.**

1 You will hear two friends talking about a new airport.
They both think that
- **A** the location is very convenient.
- **B** the recycling facilities are great.
- **C** the signs are clear.

2 You will hear a woman telling her brother about her new electric bicycle.
How does she feel about it?
- **A** not sure about how long it will last
- **B** worried about where to leave it at college
- **C** embarrassed about going to college on it

3 You will hear two colleagues talking about travelling to work.
Why does the man prefer taking the train?
- **A** He can do some work before arriving at his office.
- **B** There's nowhere to park near where he works.
- **C** Driving home in the evening takes too long.

4 You will hear two friends talking about getting to the airport.
They agree to
- **A** make a decision after doing some research.
- **B** travel to the airport together.
- **C** wait for each other at the entrance.

5 You will hear two neighbours talking about traffic in the town.
The man thinks that
- **A** the roads are confusing for visitors.
- **B** fewer cars are already coming into the town.
- **C** more changes are needed to solve the problems.

6 You will hear two friends talking about recycling.
The woman says that she
- **A** uses more glass than plastic.
- **B** finds it hard to avoid using plastic.
- **C** is careful which types of plastic she uses.

SPEAKING

1 **Read the sentences which speculate about things you can see in a picture. Choose the correct meaning for each sentence.**

1 I think the two boys must be brothers.
- **A** I'm sure they are brothers.
- **B** It's possible that they are brothers.

2 They might be on holiday.
- **A** I'm sure they are on holiday.
- **B** It's possible that they are on holiday.

3 It may not be her car.
- **A** I'm sure it isn't her car.
- **B** It's possible that it isn't her car.

4 It can't be summer.
- **A** It's possible that it's not summer.
- **B** I'm sure it isn't summer.

5 It could be some kind of meat.
- **A** It's possible that it's some kind of meat.
- **B** I'm sure it's some kind of meat.

6 It can't be in Africa.
- **A** I'm sure it's in Africa.
- **B** It isn't possible that it's in Africa.

2 **Complete the second sentence so it has a similar meaning to the first. Use a modal of speculation.**

1 I'm sure it's a rescue boat.
It _____ a rescue boat.

2 I guess it's possible that he's a teacher.
I guess he _____ a teacher.

3 I'm sure she isn't very old.
She _____ very old.

4 It's possible that he isn't pleased with his grades.
He _____ pleased with his grades.

WRITING

1 **Complete the sentences with the correct narrative tenses of the verbs.**

Last Thursday evening, I ¹*had sat / was sitting* in the *Top Pizza* restaurant on West Street, waiting for some friends. The waiter ²*came / was coming* over and asked if I wanted to order. 'No, not yet,' I ³*replied / was replying*. I ⁴*looked / was looking* at the time on my phone. It was 7.45. Where were they? We ⁵*agreed / had agreed* to meet at 7.30. While ⁶I *thought / was thinking* about what to do next, my phone ⁷*rang / was ringing*. 'Where are you?' my friend Callum ⁸*asked / had asked*. 'We're all waiting for you in the *Top Pizza* restaurant on Bridge Street!'

2 **Rewrite the direct speech sentences with the correct punctuation.**

1 nice to meet you she said
_____

2 where are you going he asked
_____

3 go away she shouted
_____

4 come with me he whispered quietly
_____

3 **Choose the best verbs for the direct speech.**

1 'Don't make too much noise,' he *whispered / cried*.
2 'Are you feeling better?' she *asked / said*.
3 'The money has gone,' he *said / told* me.
4 'You can't come in!' I *asked / shouted*.
5 'Hello!' he *told / called*.

11 A GREAT LOCATION

VOCABULARY

1 Complete the words in the people's descriptions of their homes.

> I live in a ¹t____r__c__d h_____e near the city centre. It's quite small, but it's warm and ²c_____y. It's an ³o____d-f_____n____d house, not a modern one, but I like it!

> I live in quite a big house in the ⁴s____b_____bs, about five miles from the city centre. It's a ⁵t_____-s_____r____y house, with an upstairs and a downstairs. It's a ⁶b_____d n__w house, so everything in it is very modern. It's quite close to my school, which is very ⁷c____nv____n_____t.

> I live in a tall ⁸b_____k of f_____s in the city centre, near the ⁹b____s____n____s d____st_____t where my dad works. We live on the ¹⁰t____p f_____r, so we have a great view of the city!

2 Complete the house and home quiz.

1 Where can you heat water?
   A a kettle **B** a cabinet **C** a tap

2 Where do you hang clothes?
   A a chest of drawers **B** a wardrobe **C** a cabinet

3 What do you put on your bed to keep warm?
   A a rug **B** a cushion **C** a duvet

4 Where do you put rubbish?
   A a chest of drawers **B** a rug **C** a bin

5 Where can you get water from?
   A a bin **B** a rug **C** a tap

6 What do you put on the floor to look nice?
   A a rug **B** a cushion **C** a duvet

7 Where can you keep things in a bathroom?
   A a chest of drawers **B** a bin **C** a cabinet

8 What do you put on a chair to make it more comfortable?
   A a cushion **B** a rug **C** a duvet

3 Complete the list of problems with a new flat.

> The mirror on the bathroom _____ _____ _____ _____ is cracked, so you can't see yourself very well.
>
> The _____ _____ _____ _____ isn't working properly, so the flat is cold.
>
> There's a horrible stain on the _____ _____ on the hall floor.
>
> The _____ _____ _____ _____ from the sofa are missing. It looks odd without them.
>
> One _____ _____ _____ _____ _____ and one chest of drawers aren't enough for two people. We need more space to store our clothes.
>
> The tap on the kitchen _____ _____ _____ needs fixing. We can't turn it off completely.

GRAMMAR

1 Choose the correct relative pronouns. In one sentence, both are correct.

1 Jan showed me the house *which / where* she lives.
2 The people *that / whose* I share a flat with are all really friendly.
3 This is the flat *which / who* they want to buy.
4 The friend *who / whose* flat I stayed at is called Ed.
5 The people *who / which* live next door are very nice.
6 This was a time *when / which* most people lived together in big family groups.
7 I need to make a list of all the people *who / that* I'm inviting to the housewarming party.
8 The sofa *that / who* we bought was too big.

2 Complete the sentences with the relative clauses.

> which we looked at   which is near the city centre
> which is annoying   who lives in London
> who owns our flat

1 Some of the houses _____ were too expensive for us to rent.
2 The person _____ also owns five other flats.
3 My friend Tom, _____, is mad about skateboarding.
4 Our flat, _____, is quite small and modern.
5 It takes me nearly an hour to get to school, _____.

3 Look at the relative clauses in exercise 2 again. Are they defining or non-defining? Write D or ND. In which two sentences can you use *that* instead of *which* or *who*?

1 ....   3 ....   5 ....

2 ....   4 ....

You can use *that* in sentences .... and ....

4 Read the blog post. Write the numbers of the three bold relative pronouns that you can leave out.

This is the first week in my new flat, and I love it! For a start, it's close to a big park, ¹**which** is great! It's also close to the school ²**where** I'll go in September. And my friend Sam, ³**who** I've known all my life, lives just around the corner. What could be better? The bedroom ⁴**that** I've chosen is quite big. All the things ⁵**which** I brought with me from our old flat fit in easily. The other people ⁶**who** live on our floor also seem very nice. One guy ⁷**who** I've met likes the same computer games as me, so I'm sure we'll be friends!

....

5 Join the sentences using a relative clause. Sometimes more than one relative pronoun is possible. Remember to add commas if the clause is non-defining.

1 This is the swimming pool. I use it in the summer.
This is the swimming pool ....
in the summer.

2 The new flats are expensive. They are building them in the business district.
The new flats ....
.... expensive.

3 My friend Sam lives in the suburbs. He's really sporty.
My friend Sam ....
lives in the suburbs.

4 Manchester is a great city. I live there.
Manchester ....
a great city.

5 You can use these tennis courts for free. It's amazing!
You can use these tennis courts for free
.... amazing!

6 I have met some new people. They are all very nice.
The new people ....
all very nice.

6 Rewrite the sentences using *have* or *get*.

1 Someone took our photo next to the fountain.
We ....
next to the fountain. (had)

2 I need to ask someone to fix my phone this weekend.
I need to ....
this weekend. (get)

3 Has someone cut your hair?
Have ....? (had)

4 You can ask someone to deliver your shopping to your home.
You can ....
to your home. (have)

5 It's a good idea to ask someone to check your running style before you buy new trainers.
It's a good idea to ....
.... before you buy new trainers. (get)

LISTENING

1 17 **Listen to three young people talking about where they live in London. What have they all found?**

A a clever way to meet new people and make friends
B a different way to travel to and from work cheaply
C an unusual way to live cheaply in the city

2 17 **Listen again. Which person, Ewan, Daisy, or Andy …**

1 has met other young people that they have something in common with? ....
2 doesn't have a very good bathroom? ....
3 had some problems when they first moved into their home? ....
4 is free to make changes to their home? ....
5 is going to leave their home soon? ....
6 lives close to their job? ....

For each question, choose the correct answer.

Houses that can turn around

Would you like to live in a house that follows the direction of the sun in winter and provides shade when it's really hot? This is fast becoming a **(1)** _____, as more architects around the world are designing buildings that turn around. Known as 'rotating houses', these homes are the **(2)** _____ solution for anyone who's ever **(3)** _____ like waking up to a different view from their bedroom window. And many of these houses are controlled by motors no bigger than washing machines.

Luke Everingham lives in a rotating house built with glass, metal and natural **(4)** _____ such as wood. The house is an eight-sided shape and there are eight rooms inside. Luke uses a remote control in the living room to **(5)** _____ his house turn. It takes thirty minutes to complete a full circle, so you can't **(6)** _____ it's turning unless you focus on an object outside.

1	**A**	fact	**B**	truth	**C**	reality	**D**	habit
2	**A**	great	**B**	perfect	**C**	good	**D**	fantastic
3	**A**	thought	**B**	dreamt	**C**	wanted	**D**	felt
4	**A**	materials	**B**	ingredients	**C**	contents	**D**	parts
5	**A**	make	**B**	cause	**C**	achieve	**D**	force
6	**A**	find	**B**	compare	**C**	tell	**D**	learn

PUSH YOURSELF B2

Complete the advertisements for flats to rent with adjectives.

For rent
A large double room in a
¹s _____ n _____ g
modern flat in a quiet
²r _____ d _____ t _____ l
area. The room is fully
³f _____ n _____ s _____ d, and
all bills are included in the rent.

For rent
A ⁴d _____ l _____ t _____ l
two-bedroom flat in the city centre.
Very ⁵s p _____ c _____ s,
and with a large balcony.

For rent
A ⁶u _____ i _____ e three-bedroom
flat in the business district. It has
a ⁷l _____ x _____ r _____ s
modern bathroom and
⁸p _____ c _____ r _____ s _____ e
views over the historic town centre.

SPEAKING

1 Match the beginnings and ends of the expressions you can use for showing that you are surprised. Sometimes there is more than one possible answer. There is one ending you don't need.

1 No
2 You're
3 How
4 Wow!
5 Really?

a incredible!
b I'd never have guessed that.
c way!
d joking!
e the way!
f That's unbelievable!

2 Choose the correct words to complete the description.

> We're staying in an amazing holiday flat, right by the beach. There's one big room for living in and there's, **1**____, a big glass door which opens out onto a **2**____ large balcony, where you can sit and see the sea. There's a big games room, with a table tennis table and **3**____ like that. There's **4**____ outdoor cooker where you can barbecue and cook your meals outside. And there's a shed outside with things for the beach – surfboards, small boats, those **5**____ of things. Down by the beach, there's **6**____ of natural swimming pool in the rocks, where the water's really warm – perfect!

	A		**B**		**C**	
1	**A**	kind	**B**	like	**C**	sort
2	**A**	sort	**B**	types of	**C**	kind of
3	**A**	stuff	**B**	kinds	**C**	sorts
4	**A**	a type of	**B**	a kind	**C**	like
5	**A**	stuff	**B**	like	**C**	kinds
6	**A**	type of	**B**	a sort	**C**	kind

WRITING

1 Choose the correct words to complete the sentences you can use in an email.

1 Thank you *of / for* your email.
2 Congratulations *on / for* your exam results.
3 I'm *afraid / scared* I can't come to the party.
4 Perhaps I *would / could* visit you in July?
5 I'm looking forward to *see / seeing* you soon.
6 Write *back / me* soon.

2 Complete the email with words from the box. There are some words you don't need.

best	dear	fortunately	get	getting	look
looking	love	perhaps	possible	unfortunately	

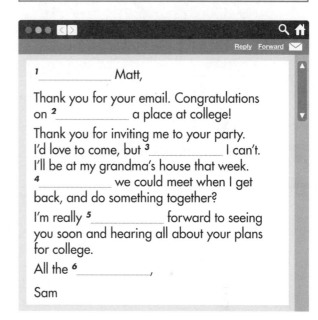

1_____ Matt,

Thank you for your email. Congratulations on **2**_____ a place at college!

Thank you for inviting me to your party. I'd love to come, but **3**_____ I can't. I'll be at my grandma's house that week. **4**_____ we could meet when I get back, and do something together?

I'm really **5**_____ forward to seeing you soon and hearing all about your plans for college.

All the **6**_____,

Sam

12 THE PERFECT JOB

VOCABULARY

1 **Read the clues and write the jobs.**

1
> Call me if you have a problem with your taps.
> p _____ _____ b _____ r

2
> I'm good at maths, and you can trust me with your money! a _____ _____ _____ _____ t _____ _____ t

3
> I help people when they have committed crimes and have to go to court. l _____ y _____ r

4
> You can come to me if you're ill and need medicines or tablets. p _____ r m _____ c _____ _____ t

5
> Call me if the lights in your house suddenly go out! e _____ _____ t r _____ c _____ _____ n

2 **What's the best job for each young person?**

architect	astronaut	lecturer
politician	programmer	

1 **John:** I think computers are amazing – and you can make them do some really cool things.
   ....

2 **Amy:** I enjoy teaching, but I'd like to teach older students, not young kids. ....

3 **Eva:** There are a lot of problems in the world, and I'd like to do something to help.
   ....

4 **Noah:** I want to see the world – from as far away as possible! ....

5 **Elsa:** I love buildings, especially modern ones with interesting designs. ....

3 **Choose the correct adjective.**

1 Maria never gets angry, even if she has to show me how to do something three times! (*creative / patient / reliable*)

2 Dan comes up with some amazing new ideas! (*organised / creative / flexible*)

3 Rob is really good at solving problems – he's so clever! (*intelligent / reliable / friendly*)

4 Abi never seems stressed, even when we're really busy. (*calm / intelligent / creative*)

5 Ollie always says hello to other people, and asks how they are. (*flexible / friendly / organised*)

6 Eva is never late, and she always finishes her work on time. (*creative / flexible / reliable*)

7 Paolo plans his work carefully, and always knows exactly what he needs to do. (*friendly / intelligent / organised*)

8 Jeni is always happy to change her plans if a situation changes. (*reliable / flexible / friendly*)

4 **Complete the tips with the words in the box.**

co-workers	director	employee
employer	freelancer	line manager
personal assistant	sales staff	

HOW TO BE HAPPY AND SUCCESSFUL AT WORK

1 Be cheerful and polite to the people you work with – your _____ don't want to work with someone who's always complaining!

2 If you have any problems, the first person to talk to is your _____ – this is the person who is directly above you in the company.

3 If you need to talk to an important person in the company, don't call them directly – talk to their _____ first, who can probably arrange an appointment for you.

4 Remember you are part of a team at work – you aren't the only _____ in the company!

5 If you have an idea for a new product, talk to the _____ – their job is to sell things and they will know if people will want to buy your idea.

6 If you are ambitious, be patient – it takes about twenty years to reach the top and become the _____ of a company!

7 Always respect the company you work for. Remember, the company is your _____ and pays you each month!

8 If you really hate working for a company, you can always leave and become a _____, working for yourself.

5 Complete the information on a careers website with the words in the box.

> certificate   communication   doctorate   good at
> good with   master's   problem-solving

Being a plumber is a great job if you like working with your hands. You can start a training course straight after high school, and at the end you will get a
¹ _____ to show you are able to do the job. You must be friendly and
² _____ people, and sometimes you have to work out the best way to do something, so you need ³ _____ skills.

To become a university lecturer, you need a bachelor's and a ⁴ _____ degree, and finally you have to spend three more years studying for a ⁵ _____. Apart from these qualifications, you also need to be
⁶ _____ presenting information, and of course you also need excellent
⁷ _____ skills so you can explain your ideas to students.

GRAMMAR

1 Choose the correct modal verbs.

A: ¹Could / Must I borrow your pen, please?

B: Yes, of course you ²could / can.

A: ³May / Couldn't I speak to Chris, please?

B: No, I'm sorry, you ⁴can't / couldn't speak to him at the moment. He's in a meeting.

A: ⁵Must / Can I eat my lunch at my desk?

B: Yes, that's fine, but you ⁶couldn't / mustn't spill food on your laptop!

A: ⁷Are we allowed to / Must we finish early on a Friday?

B: Yes, but you ⁸couldn't / can't leave before 4 p.m.

2 Look at the school rules from a school in 1900. Then complete the sentences with *had to* or the correct form of *be allowed to* and the verbs in brackets.

> All children must be in school by 8.30 a.m.
>
> Uniform is black skirts for girls and black short trousers for boys under 11, long trousers for boys over 11.
>
> Coats may be kept on in the classroom in cold weather.

In 1900, the children ¹ _____ (be) in school by 8.30 a.m. Boys under 11 years old
² _____ (wear) long trousers. Girls ³ _____ (wear) black skirts. They ⁴ _____ (keep) their coats on in the classroom in cold weather.

3 Read the sentences and choose the correct meanings.

1 My parents usually let me stay up late at the weekend.
A I can't stay up late at the weekend.
B I am allowed to stay up late at the weekend.

2 My parents make me do my homework before I can play on the computer.
A I have to do my homework first.
B I am not allowed to do my homework first.

3 My brother didn't let me borrow his bike last weekend.
A I was allowed to borrow his bike.
B I wasn't allowed to borrow his bike.

4 When I was younger, my parents made me help around the house.
A I was allowed to help around the house.
B I had to help around the house.

4 Complete the second sentence so it has a similar meaning to the first. Use the word in brackets.

1 My parents say I have to keep my bedroom tidy.
My parents _____ my bedroom tidy. (make)

2 Our teachers say we can't use our phones in class.
Our teachers _____ our phones in class. (let)

3 Her boss didn't let her go home early.
She _____ home early. (allowed)

4 My mum made me go to bed early when I was young.
I _____ early when I was young. (had)

5 Our teacher sometimes says we're allowed to look online for information.
Our teacher sometimes _____ online for information. (lets)

6 You mustn't park here.
You _____ here. (allowed)

PUSH YOURSELF B2

Complete the sentences with a modal verb and *be able to*. Sometimes more than one modal verb is possible.

1 Look, he's right there, on the other side of the room. I'm sure you can see him!
You _____ him!

2 It will be possible for you to talk to her tomorrow.
You _____ to her tomorrow.

3 It's possible that we can buy our uniforms online.
We _____ our uniforms online.

4 It's wrong that people can't camp here.
People _____ here.

5 I don't have many qualifications, so I can't get a job.
If I had more qualifications, I _____ a job.

READING

1 Match the jobs with the meanings.

1 farmer .... **2** chef .... **3** barista .... **4** childcare assistant ....

a someone who cooks food in a restaurant
b someone who uses a machine to make coffee in a café
c someone who looks after young children while their parents are working
d someone who grows crops and keeps animals to produce food

2 Read the article. Match the correct job with each paragraph.

A pharmacist   **C** farmer   **E** barista
B childcare assistant   **D** chef   **F** tour guide

ARE ROBOTS ? TAKING OUR JOBS

HOME   NEWS   ABOUT

Some people worry that robots will carry out a lot more of our jobs in the future. But is this true? Which jobs can robots do, and which jobs will they never be able to do?

1 ....
In some cafés, coffee is already served by a robot, or a robot arm at least. The arm picks up a cup, moves it to the coffee machine and presses the buttons to produce a perfect cup of coffee in about 30 seconds, which is faster than a human. Another advantage is that the robot never needs a break, and it doesn't get angry with difficult customers!

2 ....
On the other hand, if you go into a restaurant kitchen, you will find the staff are still one hundred percent human. Cooking is a creative activity, and no one has managed to produce a creative robot yet. Experts also believe that robots will never be able to cook delicious food because they can't smell or taste it.

3 ....
At one university in the United States, there is already a robot which prepares medicines for patients to collect. Doctors order the medicines online, then the robot puts the correct tablets into bottles and prints the labels. So far, the robot hasn't got anything wrong, and it is better than a human pharmacist because it can check more easily whether two medicines might not work well together.

4 ....
Robots can teach some things such as languages, but experts say they will never be able to look after young children. Young children need human contact, and they need people who can understand them. Robots can be taught to recognise behaviours, such as when someone laughs or gets angry, but they will never know when someone is upset or lonely, or scared.

5 ....
The job of growing food includes a lot of routine work which robots can definitely do. This year, a British university has completed a project to grow a complete crop hands-free, using only machines to plant it, look after it, and pick it. They now want to work towards running a whole farm using just machines.

6 ....
We now spend more and more of our working and home lives with machines. Research shows that when we're on holiday, however, we want more human contact. People who know a place well can help us to enjoy new places and new adventures in a way that is exciting and challenging for us. For this reason, humans will always be needed for this job.

3 Read the article again. Which job is each sentence about?

1 There are plans to do more work using robots in the future. ....
2 Robots are quicker and they don't get tired. ....
3 Customers want a real person to help them gain more from an experience. ....
4 This robot hasn't made a mistake yet. ....
5 Robots can't do this job because they don't have all the senses that humans have. ....
6 Robots can't do this job because they don't understand how people are feeling. ....

LISTENING PART 1

18 For each question, choose the correct answer.

1 What is the woman's job now?

 **A**  **B**  **C**

2 Which benefit does the man's company offer staff?

 **A**  **B**  **C**

3 Who works in the sales department?

 **A**  **B**  **C**

4 Where does the man work?

 **A**  **B**  **C**

5 What does the woman like best about her job?

 **A**  **B**  **C**

6 What was the man's career ambition when he was a child?

 **A**  **B**  **C**

7 Who is the woman's sister?

 **A**  **B**  **C**

SPEAKING

1 **Complete the conversations with words from the box. There are some words you don't need.**

agree	disagree	exactly	I'd
I'm	perhaps	right	sorry

1 **A:** I think that politicians should be paid more.

   B: _____, but I don't agree. They get quite enough already!

2 **A:** We need to encourage more people to become teachers.

   B: _____! We really need more teachers.

3 **A:** Nurses should get the same salary as doctors.

   B: I'm afraid I _____. Doctors have to train for many years.

4 **A:** Firefighters do a very dangerous job.

   B: Yes, you're right. _____ agree with that.

2 **Choose the correct expression.**

1 **A:** I think George would be a brilliant politician!

   B: *Sorry, but I don't agree. / Yes, you're right.* He really wants to make people's lives better.

2 **A:** I think working as a programmer would be fun.

   B: *Exactly! / I don't think that's true.* I think a lot of their work must be really quite boring!

3 **A:** It's easy to become an electrician!

   B: *I agree with you. / I'm afraid I disagree.* You need to do a lot of training, actually.

4 **A:** I think it must be amazing to be an astronaut.

   B: *Perhaps, but it's not all fun. / I'd agree with that.* It must be great to look down at the Earth!

WRITING

Complete the job advertisement.

applicants	application	full-time	must
opportunity	qualifications	should be able	

MAGIC ASSISTANT

Why not become a magic assistant? This is a great
¹_____ for someone who enjoys being on the stage and wants to try something different! This is a ²_____ job, starting next month.

³_____ should be 18 years old and in good health. They ⁴_____ to make decisions quickly and keep smiling when things go wrong. They ⁵_____ be brave and able to hide their fear! There are no ⁶_____ necessary for this job – we will consider anyone who loves magic shows!

Please send your ⁷_____ to jojomagic@magicshows.org.

13 GET INVOLVED!

VOCABULARY

1 Complete what the people say about sport with the correct form of the verbs in brackets. There is one verb in each group that you don't need.

> I decided last year that I should **1**_____ a new sport, so I **2**_____ my local tennis club. I love it! I'm much healthier now and I even **3**_____ the club in matches from time to time!
> (*hold / join / represent / take up*)

> I do athletics, but just for fun. I don't often **4**_____ in competitions. I don't want to take it too seriously because I also enjoy **5**_____ at the weekend. It's fun when I **6**_____ my friends in races, though!
> (*beat / go out / represent / take part*)

> I love football! I **7**_____ my local team and I go to all their games. Last year, the club **8**_____ a competition to find the most loyal fan, and I was in the top ten! I sometimes play football with my friends, but I've never **9**_____ a goal!
> (*hold / score / support / take up*)

2 Complete the crossword.

```
          ¹C
 ²O ▢ ▢ ▢ ▢ ▢ ▢ ▢
          ▢
    ³S ▢ P ▢ ▢ ▢ ▢ ▢ ▢
          ▢
       ⁴T ▢ ▢ ▢ ▢ ▢ ▢ ▢ ▢ ▢
          ▢
 ⁵S ▢ ▢ ▢ ▢ ▢ ▢ ▢ ▢
          O
 ⁶R ▢ ▢ ▢ ▢ ▢
```

Across

2 the people you play against in a sport
3 people who watch a team and want them to win
4 the people you play in a game or competition with
5 someone who watches a sports event live, in a stadium
6 the person who decides if players are following the rules

Down

1 someone who takes part in a competition

3 Complete what the people say with *do, play* or *go*.

★ HAVE YOUR SAY
What's your sporting dream?

> I'd like to **1**_____ running in the desert – what a challenge! **Emma, 16**

> I'd like to be fit enough to climb a mountain and then **2**_____ a workout at the top! **Erica, 15**

> I want to **3**_____ ice skating on a frozen lake in Canada – cool! **Stella, 16**

> I'd love to **4**_____ basketball with one of the great American teams – but I'll never be tall enough! **Paul, 15**

> I'd like to **5**_____ yoga on an empty beach in the Caribbean – just me, the sea and the sand! **Rose, 15**

> Tennis is my favourite sport, so of course my dream is to **6**_____ tennis at Wimbledon! **Matt, 14**

> I'd love to **7**_____ karate at a high level – cut through wood with my hands, that kind of thing! **Connor, 15**

4 Complete the quiz with the words in the box. Then do the quiz and check your answers on page 59.

course	court	rink	pitch	pool	ramp	track

SPORTS TRIVIA – test your knowledge!

1 The biggest natural ice skating _____ is the Rideau Canal in *Canada / Russia*. It is 7.8 km long.

2 The most footballs you can get on a football _____ is over *50,000 / 150,000*!

3 The deepest swimming _____ is in Italy and is *32 / 42* metres deep. It is used for diving.

4 The oldest ball boy to collect balls on a tennis _____ during an official match was *82 / 92*.

5 The oldest golf _____ in the world is in *the USA / Scotland*, where the sport started.

6 Yiannis Kouros holds the record for the longest distance that anyone has run on an athletics _____ in 24 hours. In 1997, Yiannis ran *202 / 303* km.

7 The fastest speed anyone has ever done on a skateboard wasn't on a skateboard _____, but on the road. The speed is *146 / 166* kilometres an hour.

GRAMMAR

1 Complete the sentences with the gerund form of the verbs in the box.

> buy   climb   dive   run
> join   meet   practise   spend

1 _____ to the top of a really high mountain must be an amazing experience!

2 I love _____ time with my cousins – we always have a laugh together.

3 I fancy _____ a sports club, but I'm not sure which sport to choose.

4 If you want to become good at any sport, you need to keep _____!

5 My uncle is mad about _____ – he does five km every morning!

6 I've never tried _____ because I hate being under water.

7 It's worth _____ a ticket to a professional football match if you love the sport.

8 My brother is keen on _____ other people who want to play chess.

2 Complete the sentences. Use *to* and the infinitive.

1 I think it _____ (be / important / do) exercise every day.

2 Maria _____ (learn / swim) last year.

3 I _____ (can't wait / take part) in my first judo competition.

4 Sasha loves music and she _____ (want / try) salsa dancing.

5 We were losing 2–0, but we finally _____ (manage / win) 3–2.

6 Hello. It _____ (be / nice / meet) you.

7 Last week, Sam _____ (persuade / me / go) skateboarding with him.

8 I'm often stressed, so I _____ (do / yoga / relax) in the evenings.

9 Max won two tickets for the cup final, so he _____ (invite / me / go) with him.

10 I needed a new belt, so I _____ (go / into town / buy) one.

3 Complete the text with the verbs in brackets. Use the gerund or *to* and the infinitive.

DO SOMETHING DIFFERENT!

1 _____ (spend) time on or near water is always fun, and most people enjoy **2** _____ (try) new sports. So why not have a go at wakeboarding? Wakeboarding is like skateboarding, only on water. There are plenty of places where you can do it, so you can look online **3** _____ (find) a place near you. We advise people **4** _____ (have) a few lessons so they can learn the basic skills. It's possible **5** _____ (hire) a board at first, but it's worth **6** _____ (buy) your own board as you get better, so you can practise **7** _____ (do) more difficult moves. Wakeboarding can be dangerous, so it's important **8** _____ (wear) a helmet. We also recommend **9** _____ (wear) a wetsuit **10** _____ (keep) you warm.

LISTENING PART 3

 19 For each question, write the correct answer in the gap.

Write one or two words or a number or a date or a time.

You will hear a gym owner called Lee Norton talking about a spin class.

> **New Spin Class with VR (Virtual Reality)**
>
> Lee's gym introduced the VR spin class in **(1)** _____.
>
> Lee says the new VR spin class mixes exercise with **(2)** _____.
>
> When Lee tried the class himself, he found exercising less **(3)** _____.
>
> Lee says he most enjoys the VR session involving cycling through the **(4)** _____.
>
> The best class for beginners is **(5)** _____ long.
>
> Lee has plans for a VR class which offers the experience of **(6)** _____.

1 Read the article. Choose the best summary.

A Joe Fuller still loves surfing in spite of a terrible experience.

B Joe Fuller explains why surfing is an ideal sport for anyone who enjoys excitement and danger.

C Joe Fuller encourages other surfers to learn from his experience and be more careful.

2 Read the article again. Decide if the sentences are true or false. Correct the false sentences.

1 Joe started surfing as soon as he moved to the coast.

2 Joe says he loves surfing mainly because of how he feels when it goes well.

3 When Joe was carried out to sea, he wasn't sure what he should do.

4 Joe felt grateful when he was rescued, but also disappointed about losing his surfboard.

5 Joe had no fears about surfing again after his accident.

Choose the correct words to complete the comments about Joe's story.

sporty_jill
Wow! What an amazing story. It really cheered me ¹*up / out* to read about how brave Joe is! I think he should definitely stick ²*for / at* his surfing and enjoy it!

dunc_rose
Reading about Joe made me want to ³*take / have* a go at surfing myself, though I'm sure I won't ⁴*learn / pick* it up very quickly!

seeseaemily
I ⁵*got / made* into surfing a few years ago. I love it, but reading Joe's story has made me wonder if I should just chill ⁶*up / out* on the beach instead, where it's safe!

andy_surf
Great story! Surfing is an amazing sport, once you ⁷*get / take* the hang of it. It's a great way to wind ⁸*down / off* when you're stressed. Yes, it can be dangerous, and that's why beginners should never go out surfing on their own. Hope you're reading this, Joe!

HOME **STORIES** ABOUT

MAD ABOUT SURFING

Joe Fuller can still clearly remember the first day he tried surfing. He was 14 years old. He'd moved to the coast two years before but wasn't very interested in sport at that time. Then some of his friends suggested going surfing one day in the summer holidays and he said yes. And that was it – he fell in love with the sport!

Joe says it's hard to describe what he thinks is so special about surfing. Obviously, it's wonderful to see the way the sea changes each day, so there are always new challenges to try. But according to Joe, the best thing is the amazing sense of freedom that you get when you're riding the perfect wave!

But last year Joe had a terrifying experience. While he was surfing alone, the waves carried him out to sea, instead of bringing him back to the shore. Joe knew that it might be some time before rescuers found him, and he knew the dangers of being in cold water for too long. But he also knew he had no choice but to stay with his surfboard and wait. Rescuers found him 16 hours later, nearly 20 kilometres away from the coast! He was cold and hungry, but still alive!

Joe says he can remember the mixture of feelings he had after he was rescued. He was exhausted, of course, and also quite upset that there wasn't room in the rescue helicopter to bring his surfboard with him! But most of all he couldn't wait to thank all the people who had worked so hard to find him and save his life.

And how did he feel about surfing again after his accident? He admits that he was a little nervous about getting into the water again, but once he rode his first wave the old excitement came back and he knew that stopping just wasn't an option!

SPEAKING

1 Choose the correct words to complete the sentences.

1 I love rugby, *so / since* I watch a lot of rugby matches on TV.

2 I live near the sea, *because / which is why* it's easy for me to do water sports.

3 *So / Because* I'm quite a sociable person, I prefer team sports to individual sports.

4 I'm going to watch an athletics competition on Saturday, *since / so* I'm a big fan of athletics.

5 *As / So* I don't have much money, I can't afford to join a gym.

6 I love tennis *which is why / because* it's a really exciting sport.

2 Two people are discussing the idea of building a gym. Complete the mini-dialogues with the correct words. There are two words you don't need.

agree	am	do	don't	how	really	right
should	sure	that's	think	what's		

A: I think it would be good idea to build a gym in the town. ¹_____ your opinion?

B: I ²_____ with you. A gym would be a great idea.

A: I think they ³_____ open a café at the gym. What ⁴_____ you think?

B: Yes, you're ⁵_____. I think ⁶_____ a good idea.

A: ⁷_____ about an outdoor gym in the park?

B: ⁸_____? I'm not ⁹_____ that's the best idea.

A: I think that most gyms are too expensive.

B: I ¹⁰_____ agree with you. Some gyms are quite cheap, especially for students.

WRITING

1 Read the article about someone's favourite sport. Choose the best topic sentence for each paragraph. There is one topic sentence you don't need.

A I first started climbing five years ago. ....

B Some of my friends think that climbing is too dangerous. ....

C My favourite sport is climbing. ....

D Climbing can be done by people of any age. ....

1 It's a popular sport all over the world. Some people climb high mountains with ropes to keep them safe. Other people prefer low climbing with no ropes. You can also practise the sport in some climbing gyms.

2 Some friends invited me to go to the climbing gym with them. I enjoyed it, so I decided to take it up. Since then, I've joined a climbing club and next year I'm going climbing in France with the club.

3 Young children can start from the age of four or five, and people can continue climbing when they're quite old. In fact, climbing is a very good way to stay fit and strong all through your life. Climbing is a great sport for everyone!

2 Choose the correct linkers in the sentences.

1 Tennis is a fun sport to play. It's *too / also* a very exciting sport to watch.

2 I love singing *but / because* it always makes me feel cheerful.

3 I play *both / and* the guitar and the piano.

4 Last summer I went to some drama workshops, *which / and* I enjoyed a lot.

5 Dancing is a great way to keep fit. It's really good fun *too / also*.

6 I love acting, *but / because* I always get really nervous before a show.

3 Correct one spelling error in each sentence.

1 They forgot to bring there sports kit with them. ....

2 I love painting and I think its an amazing hobby. ....

3 I don't no where the swimming pool is. ....

4 There are a lot of sports facilities hear. ....

5 When you're watching birds, you have to be very quite and not make any noise. ....

6 You don't have to by a lot of equipment to play football. ....

Answers to quiz on page 56
1 Canada 2 150,000 3 42 4 82 5 Scotland 6 303 7 146

14 ON TOP OF THE WORLD

VOCABULARY

1 Choose the correct adjectives.

1 I was really *disappointed / delighted* when my team lost the game.
2 We were all really *amused / shocked* when we saw how much damage the storm had done.
3 I always get really *satisfied / nervous* before exams.
4 I think we should do something to make Emma laugh. She looks really *miserable / impressed*!
5 It's important to talk to someone about your problems if you feel *depressed / jealous*.

2 Complete the blog post with the words in the box.

| cheerful | embarrassed | guilty | impressed | jealous |

DO YOUR FEELINGS EVER ANNOY YOU?

Mine do. For example, when a friend has done really well I want to feel pleased for him, and ¹ _____ with his achievement, but I can't help feeling just a little bit ² _____ of his success. Or when I see someone slip on the ice, sometimes I can't help laughing and then I feel really ³ _____ because it's wrong to be mean! Or I might do something silly when other people are watching, so I feel really ⁴ _____ and it spoils my ⁵ _____ mood. Wouldn't it be great if we could control our feelings?

3 Read the descriptions of four people and choose two adjectives to complete each one.

1 Matt's often _____ to people and he treats animals badly too. He can be quite _____ to his dog. (*cute / cruel / patient / rude*)
2 Conor never thinks before he does things, so he does some really _____ things, but he's really kind and _____ – he always buys me nice presents! (*cute / fashionable / generous / stupid*)
3 Your little sister has lovely big eyes – she's so _____ ! I love her long, _____ hair, too! (*clear / curly / cute / stupid*)
4 Reece is really _____ – he's never afraid to try new things, even if they're a bit dangerous. He's also very _____ with his annoying little sister! (*brave / stupid / patient / rude*)

GRAMMAR

1 Complete the conditional sentences with the correct form of the verbs in brackets.

1 Dan is always in a bad mood if he _____ (lose) at computer games.
2 If you are rude to Sam, he _____ (not invite) you to his party!
3 If Alice wasn't such a difficult person, more people _____ (like) her.
4 I'd be delighted if I _____ (get) 90% in a maths test!
5 I'll call you if I _____ (manage) to get tickets.

2 Report the conversations.

Adam: Where are you going?
Lia: I'm going home.
1 Adam asked Lia _____ .
2 Lia said that she _____ home.

Ella: Have you finished your project?
Paul: No, but I want to finish it by Friday.
3 Ella asked Paul _____ .
4 Paul said no, but he _____ by Friday.

Ana: Why did Emma leave the party?
Amy: I don't know.
5 Ana asked Amy why _____ .
6 Amy said that she _____ .

Laura: Is Tom OK?
Alex: I'm not sure. I'll talk to him.
7 Laura asked Alex _____ .
8 Alex said that he _____ sure, and he said he _____ to him.

3 Complete the relative clauses in the joined sentences. Use *who, which, where* or *whose*.

1 It's important to thank people. They help you.
It's important to thank people _____ .
2 Jen showed me the house. She grew up there.
Jen showed me the house _____ .
3 Tyler has offered to help with the food for the party. His dad is a chef.
Tyler, _____ , has offered to help with the food for the party.
4 The hotel was huge. We stayed in it.
The hotel _____ .
5 I passed the exam. I was delighted about it.
I passed the exam, _____ about.

4 Choose the correct modal verbs.

GOT A PROBLEM?
Maybe we can help!

I feel tired all the time and I ¹*can't / couldn't / shouldn't* stay awake at school. I know I ²*must / ought / should* to get to bed earlier, but I keep getting messages from friends! **Lydia, 15**

Teen Talk's advice: You definitely ³*should / need / might* get more sleep. If you're too tired, your brain isn't ⁴*able / allowed / let* to work properly. We know it ⁵*should / can't / must* be difficult for you, but remember, you really ⁶*need to / must / don't have to* answer messages immediately! You ⁷*can / can't / might* find it useful to leave your phone in the kitchen overnight.

My parents won't ⁸*let / allow / make* me go out with my friends at the weekend. They say I ⁹*must / could / have* to help with our family restaurant. We keep arguing about it. What can I do? **Dean, 16**

Teen Talk's advice: Talk to them calmly and explain that you are almost an adult and they ¹⁰*shouldn't / can't / need to* give you a bit more freedom.

READING

Read the article. Choose the correct answers.

1 According to the writer,
A we often experience more than one feeling in the same moment.
B words are often more complicated than feelings.

2 In paragraph 2, the writer says that
A there are too many different words for feelings.
B sometimes words for feelings may be missing in our language.

3 You feel *myötähäpeä*
A when you feel bad because you have done something foolish.
B when you feel bad for another person.

4 *Iktsuarpok* is a feeling you get
A when you are waiting for something bad to happen.
B when you are looking forward to something.

5 Computers can already
A help people to communicate through their minds.
B see and understand people's feelings.

6 According to the writer, in the future
A computers may help us to put our feelings into words.
B we may not need to use words to communicate our feelings.

FEELINGS WITHOUT WORDS?

When someone asks you how you're feeling, do you sometimes find it hard to choose the right word to explain? That's not surprising, because feelings are complicated things, and the words we use to describe them often seem too simple. For example, how do you feel when you fail an exam or lose a sports competition? Disappointed? Angry? Embarrassed? Scared? The chances are, you feel all of these things at the same time and there's no word that *really* describes what's going on in your head.

People have always found it difficult to put feelings into words, and sometimes what you're feeling may not even have a word in your language. There are lots of different words for feelings in different languages, like the Finnish word *myötähäpeä*, for example. This describes the feeling you get when you see someone else doing something silly, and you feel embarrassed for them! Or there's the Danish word *hygge*, which means that lovely warm feeling you get when you sit around the fire with good friends on a cold winter's evening. Or what about the Inuit word *iktsuarpok,* which is that feeling of excitement you get when you're expecting someone to arrive at your house, and you can't stop looking out of the window to see if they're coming. We recognise all these feelings, but of course it's hard to explain them if our own language doesn't have a word for them.

In the future, however, things might become easier. Scientists are working on computer systems that can 'read' people's thoughts. The computer 'watches' the electrical activity in someone's brain and then changes this into a digital message, which can be sent to another person. Scientists in Spain have already managed to send the thought 'hello' from one brain to another in this way. So, it's possible that in the future, when someone asks you how you're feeling, you might be able to turn a switch so that they can feel exactly what you're feeling, with no need to put it into words!

Complete the sentences with compound adjectives formed from the words in brackets.

1 There are nine _____ students in my class. (blue / eyes)

2 Joe's dad is a _____ artist. (respect / highly)

3 She's now got a very _____ job. (pay / well)

4 My grandad may be old, but he's still very _____. (open / mind)

5 I saw an old photo of my dad when he was a _____ student! (long / hair)

6 This is a _____ film, so we should go and see it. (recommend / highly)

 20 **For each question, choose the correct answer.**

You will hear an interview with a musician called Molly Ford talking about growing up with famous parents.

1 Molly first realised her parents were famous when
  A her family were followed by photographers.
  B she saw her parents' picture in a magazine.
  C fans stopped her parents in the street.

2 Although Molly enjoyed going on tour with her parents, she missed
  A her friends.
  B her daily routine.
  C her room at home.

3 How did Molly feel when she read articles about her parents?
  A angry because they said unpleasant things
  B pleased because she was mentioned in them
  C proud because so many people liked her parents

4 Molly remembers her parents often telling her that being famous
  A can have several advantages.
  B is never a permanent situation.
  C prevents you from having a normal life.

5 What does Molly say about her parents' famous friends?
  A They tell her lots of things about their lives.
  B They are just normal people to her.
  C They act differently in private and in public.

6 Molly think that if she has children in the future, she will
  A give up performing.
  B go travelling with them.
  C ask her parents to look after them.

SPEAKING

1 Complete the questions with the words in the box.

> can   do   how   is   long
> often   which   why

1 .... do you usually get to school?

2 .... you swim?

3 How .... do you go shopping?

4 .... you prefer to play sport or watch it?

5 How .... have you known your best friend?

6 .... it important to do exercise every week?

7 .... do you enjoy going on holiday?

8 .... is more fun, going to the cinema or watching a movie at home?

2 Choose the best answer to each question in exercise 1.

1 **A** I sometimes walk, or I get the bus if I'm late.
   B I usually get to school at half past eight.

2 **A** No, I don't like swimming in the sea, but I like going to the swimming pool.
   B Yes, I can. I'm quite a good swimmer.

3 **A** I usually go with my friends because they help me to choose new clothes.
   B I don't go every week, but I go about once a month.

4 **A** I'm quite sporty, so I prefer to play sports myself.
   B I like football and tennis, and I often watch them on TV.

5 **A** His name is James, and he's 15 years old, like me.
   B I first met him when I was five, so I've known him for about 10 years.

6 **A** I think it's very important to do regular exercise, to keep fit and healthy.
   B I go running every week because I think it's a good kind of exercise.

7 **A** I like it because when I'm on holiday I feel completely relaxed.
   B I usually go to the beach and lie in the sun or swim in the sea.

8 **A** I often watch movies with my friends at home because we all like the same kinds of movies.
   B I prefer to go to the cinema because films look more exciting on a big screen.

WRITING

1 Look at the student's paragraph plan for a profile of a friend. Then read sentences A–H and decide which two sentences should go in each paragraph (1–4).

> ### Profile of Lily
>
> 1 her life and family   ....
> 2 her appearance   ....
> 3 her personality   ....
> 4 things we do together   ....

A She's very kind and friendly, and loves meeting new people.

B We sometimes watch films or play computer games together.

C She's quite tall, and she's got fair, curly hair.

D Lily is my cousin and she lives in Amsterdam.

E Usually when we get together we just chat for hours!

F She loves clothes, so she always wears smart, fashionable clothes.

G She's also very intelligent and she wants to study medicine at university.

H Her family moved there when she was three.

2 Read another student's profile of a friend. Choose the correct words to complete it.

Sarah is my best friend. She was born in France, [1]but / when she moved to London with her family when she was seven years old. Now she goes to the same school as me, [2]so / because I see her every day.

[3]Although / However Sarah and I go to the same school, we are very different. Sarah has short, fair hair and wears very fashionable clothes. She's [4]too / also very intelligent, and she wants to study business at university.

[5]However / So, Sarah doesn't only think about herself and her career. She's very kind and generous, and she loves doing things to help other people.

We always have fun [6]because / when we meet up. Sometimes we cook a meal together, [7]as well / or we watch a film and then talk about it afterwards. I love talking to Sarah [8]because / so she always has something interesting to say!

ANSWER KEY

STARTER

VOCABULARY

Exercise 1

1 music
2 travel
3 fashion
4 cooking
5 sports
6 arts and crafts

Exercise 2

1 listening
2 playing
3 buying
4 cooking
5 making
6 learning

Exercise 3

1 up
2 have
3 have
4 go
5 have
6 up
7 out
8 out
9 out

Exercise 4

1 sales assistant
2 chef
3 journalist
4 gardener
5 police officer
6 mechanic
7 hairdresser

GRAMMAR

Exercise 1

1 never gets up
2 'm enjoying
3 usually earn
4 is always borrowing
5 are becoming
6 are often
7 'm not reading
8 doesn't like
9 is always telling
10 isn't working

Exercise 2

1 Where
2 Who
3 When
4 How
5 What
6 Why
1 d
2 a
3 e
4 f
5 c
6 b

Exercise 3

1 What are you doing?
2 What time does the film start?
3 Who is Max talking to?
4 Are they going home now?
5 Does Sam work in a restaurant?
6 What do you usually have for breakfast?

Exercise 4

1 'm studying
2 am usually
3 do the weekends go
4 sometimes go
5 is always borrowing
6 have
7 'm training
8 hate

LISTENING

Exercise 1

1 cookery vlogger
2 tennis player
3 journalist

Exercise 2

1 Maria
2 Anika
3 Sam
4 Sam
5 Maria
6 Anika

Exercise 3

1 in
2 as
3 at
4 to
5 for
6 for

READING

Exercise 1

1 b
2 g
3 a
4 d
5 f
6 c

Exercise 2

1 false
2 true
3 true
4 false
5 false
6 true

Exercise 3

1 it's worth it
2 employ
3 light
4 traditional
5 challenge
6 culture

SPEAKING

Exercise 1

1 What's your name?
2 Nice to meet you.
3 Where are you from?
4 What do you do?
5 How are you?
6 Do you like listening to music?

Exercise 2

a 3
b 1
c 6
d 5
e 4
f 2

Exercise 3

1 B
2 A
3 B
4 A
5 B
6 A

WRITING

Exercise 1

1 c
2 f
3 g
4 a
5 e
6 b
7 d

Exercise 2

1 18 **years** old
2 At the moment I'm **studying**
3 to become **a** police officer
4 My classes **usually start** at
5 I **am always** tired
6 I enjoy **hanging** out with my friends

UNIT 1

VOCABULARY

Exercise 1

1 i
2 b
3 c
4 a
5 f
6 e
7 h
8 d
9 g

Exercise 2

1 B
2 A
3 B
4 C
5 A

Exercise 3

1 cool
2 dull
3 climate
4 damp
5 lightning
6 chilly

Exercise 4

1 sunshine
2 humid
3 showers
4 breeze
5 fine
6 chilly

GRAMMAR

Exercise 1

1 cheapest
2 best
3 more expensive
4 smaller
5 more crowded
6 biggest
7 most comfortable
8 noisier
9 most enjoyable

Exercise 2

2 less crowded
3 isn't as expensive
4 beautiful as
5 is less interesting

Exercise 3

1 too cold
2 clean enough
3 too expensive
4 big enough
5 enough time

Exercise 4

1 so
2 such a
3 such a
4 so
5 such a

Exercise 5

1 such
2 more
3 so
4 as hot as
5 warm enough
6 too
7 most
8 less
9 biggest
10 cheaper

PUSH YOURSELF B2

1 climate change
2 environmentally friendly
3 carbon footprint
4 waste
5 fossil fuels
6 conservation

LISTENING

Exercise 1

C

Exercise 2

1 false
2 false
3 true
4 true
5 true
6 false

READING PART 2

1 G
2 F
3 D
4 E
5 B

SPEAKING

Exercise 1

1 O
2 D
3 A
4 S
5 A
6 O
7 S
8 D

Exercise 2

1 might
2 think
3 best
4 afraid
5 enjoy
6 opinion
7 great

Exercise 3

1 Perhaps they could
2 That's true.
3 I think they'd enjoy
4 Yes, you're right.
5 What do you think?
6 I'm afraid I disagree with you.

Exercise 4

1 A
2 B
3 B
4 A
5 B

WRITING

Exercise 1

1 Although
2 What's more
3 too
4 and
5 As well as
6 but

Exercise 2

1 and
2 also
3 Although
4 As well as
5 too
6 though

UNIT 2

VOCABULARY

1 soundtrack
2 bestseller
3 audience
4 thriller
5 episode
6 comedy
7 stage
Extra word: documentary

GRAMMAR

Exercise 1

1 've (have) never been
2 went
3 's (has) always loved
4 seemed
5 sang
6 accepted
7 hasn't done
8 've (have) never seen

Exercise 2

1 Did you enjoy the concert last Saturday; did
2 Have you ever acted in a play; have
3 Did you go to any festivals last summer; didn't
4 Has Paul seen the new *Star Wars* film yet; has
5 Did Freya win the singing competition last week; did
6 Have your friends ever organised a surprise party for you; haven't

Exercise 3

1 college since
2 the café for
3 tablet since
4 Laura for
5 in dance since
6 this house for

Exercise 4

1 yet
2 yet
3 already
4 already
5 yet
6 yet

Exercise 5

1 used to be
2 didn't use to speak
3 used to play
4 did they use to do
5 didn't use to happen
6 used to perform

LISTENING PART 2

1 B
2 A
3 C
4 C
5 A
6 C

READING

Exercise 1

B

Exercise 2

1 haven't changed
2 can imagine they are
3 looked disappointing
4 they look more realistic
5 People of all ages

PUSH YOURSELF B2

1 A
2 B
3 C
4 B
5 A
6 C
7 B
8 C

SPEAKING

1 stand
2 thing
3 fan
4 crazy
5 into
6 mind

WRITING

Exercise 1

1 Hi
2–3 Hi, Dear
4 Bye
5 See
6 Looking; to seeing

Exercise 2

2 Where's
3 I'll
4 I'd love
5 That's
6 Jack's

Exercise 3

1 Would
2 could
3 Sorry, but
4 going
5 That's
6 meet
7 don't we

Exercise 4

1 I
2 S
3 R
4 S
5 R
6 S
7 S

UNIT 3

VOCABULARY

Exercise 1

1 meal
2 bowl
3 starter
4 dish
5 course
6 plate
7 bill
8 tip
Question: dessert

Exercise 2

1 B
2 C
3 A
4 B
5 C
6 C
7 A
8 C

Exercise 3

1 Fry
2 Add
3 Mix
4 heat
5 put
6 pour
7 Grate

GRAMMAR

Exercise 1

1 absolutely
2 quite
3 really
4 absolutely
5 extremely
6 really

Exercise 2

1 little
2 any
3 few
4 much
5 no

Exercise 3

1 many
2 few
3 some / a
4 much
5 any
6 little
7 lot
8 an

Exercise 4

1 a few
2 any
3 lot
4 a little
5 a few

Exercise 5

1	Ø	5	Ø
2	a	6	the
3	the	7	Ø
4	an	8	a

Exercise 6

1 Ø
2 many
3 a
4 a
5 a lot of
6 the
7 the
8 any

LISTENING

Exercise 1

A

Exercise 2

1	A	4	C
2	B	5	C
3	B	6	A

READING PART 4

1 C
2 H
3 D
4 A
5 G

PUSH YOURSELF B2

Exercise 1

1 It's a piece of cake.
2 It's not my cup of tea.
3 I'd take it with a pinch of salt.
4 He spilt the beans.
5 It's all gone pear-shaped.
6 It's no good crying over spilt milk.

Exercise 2

a	6
b	1
c	5
d	4
e	3
f	2

SPEAKING

Exercise 1

1 not sure
2 behind
3 on
4 is holding
5 like
6 because
7 at

Exercise 2

1 c
2 a
3 f
4 b
5 d
6 e

WRITING

Exercise 1

1 last
2 When
3 At
4 After
5 end
6 later

Exercise 2

1 last Saturday
2 When they arrived
3 then
4 After a while
5 at first
6 Next
7 At the end of the evening

UNIT 4

VOCABULARY

Exercise 1

1 stream
2 neighbourhood
3 apartment block
4 waterfall
5 skyscraper
6 valley

Exercise 2

1 signposts
2 subway
3 food truck
4 skyline
5 nature
6 scenery

Exercise 3

1 c
2 d
3 e
4 f
5 a
6 b

GRAMMAR

Exercise 1

1 was raining
2 arrived
3 ran
4 rang
5 was waiting
6 checked
7 was thinking
8 saw

Exercise 2

1 arrived while I was having a shower.
2 was waiting for the bus when he saw Sam.
3 met Paul while/when she was living in London.

Exercise 3

1 had already started
2 had just left
3 had never tried
4 Had you ever visited

Exercise 4

1 went
2 had never visited
3 looked
4 found
5 had built
6 had
7 had learned/learnt
8 managed

READING

Exercise 1

B

Exercise 2

1	B
2	C
3	A
4	B
5	C
6	B

LISTENING PART 1

1 B
2 C
3 C
4 A
5 B
6 C
7 B

PUSH YOURSELF B2

1 took
2 was staying
3 got
4 hadn't brought
5 ran
6 were walking
7 spent
8 had forgotten

SPEAKING

Exercise 1

1 about
2 sounds
3 Shall
4 sure
5 could
6 idea
7 that's
8 Let's
9 like
10 better

Exercise 2

1 B
2 C
3 C
4 B
5 A
6 C

WRITING

Exercise 1

1 next
2 after
3 end
4 first
5 later
6 when

Exercise 2

1 While
2 then
3 after that
4 Later
5 finally

UNIT 5

VOCABULARY

Exercise 1

1 skin
2 knee
3 bone
4 lung
5 wrist
6 ankle
7 muscle
8 tongue
9 shoulder
10 elbow

Exercise 2

1 ill
2 cold
3 sore throat
4 cough
5 earache
6 backache

Exercise 3

1 injure
2 painful
3 hurt
4 sore
5 injury

Exercise 4

1 patients
2 prescription
3 tablets
4 emergency
5 infection

GRAMMAR

Exercise 1

1 couldn't dive
2 could ski
3 is able to walk
4 wasn't able to finish
5 can't run

Exercise 2

1 do
2 ought to
3 eat
4 ought to
5 shouldn't

Exercise 3
1. A
2. B
3. C
4. C
5. A
6. A
7. A
8. C

Exercise 4
1. must have
2. don't need to book
3. mustn't use
4. have to ask
5. don't have to bring
6. need to know

Exercise 5
1. aren't able
2. has to
3. must
4. can
5. don't need to
6. should
7. ought to
8. mustn't

PUSH YOURSELF B2
1. g
2. c
3. e
4. h
5. b
6. a
7. d
8. f

READING PART 6
1. never/not
2. there
3. a
4. it
5. do
6. at

LISTENING

Exercise 1
D

Exercise 2
1. false
2. false
3. true
4. true
5. false
6. false
7. true
8. false
9. true

SPEAKING

Exercise 1
1. g
2. c
3. a
4. e
5. h
6. f
7. b
8. d

Exercise 2
1. how are
2. feel better
3. matter
4. sorry to hear
5. I were you
6. Poor
7. Why don't you
8. look after

WRITING

Exercise 1
1. muscle
2. appointment
3. middle
4. backache
5. tongue
6. knee
7. healthy
8. breathe

Exercise 2
Punctuation: don't, I'm, You're, He's, I've, it's really good
Prepositions: Thanks **for**, worry **about** me, good **for** me, looked **after** me
Modal verbs: I should still rest, I can't remember

UNIT 6

VOCABULARY

Exercise 1
Across:
2. post
6. follow
7. request
8. tag
Down:
1. block
3. selfie
4. comment
5. update

Exercise 2
1. unfriended
2. story
3. status
4. filters
5. update
6. requests

Exercise 3
1. broke
2. grew
3. make
4. turn
5. hit
6. rely
7. get

GRAMMAR

Exercise 1
1. are you going to move
2. 'll help
3. Is Harry going to come
4. 'll text
5. 'm going to do
6. 'll lend

Exercise 2
1. 're going; starts
2. are you doing
3. leaves
4. 'm meeting
5. closes
6. Are you seeing

Exercise 3
1. 'm going to miss
2. will be; won't travel
3. 's going to rain
4. won't need; will drive
5. will ever live
6. 's going to pass

Exercise 4
1. starts
2. 's going to be
3. 'm going to work
4. 'm meeting
5. 'll have
6. 'm going to stop
7. 'm not going to check
8. 'll start

LISTENING PART 3
1. university
2. selfies
3. 2/two hours
4. novel
5. stressed
6. news

READING

Exercise 1
A. 3
B. 5
C. 1
D. 4

Exercise 2
1. B
2. A
3. C
4. C
5. D
6. A
7. D
8. B

PUSH YOURSELF B2
1. will probably travel
2. doubt (that) machines will
3. good chance (that) computers will
4. certainly won't stop
5. not much chance that
6. will definitely eat

SPEAKING

Exercise 1
1. B
2. A
3. B
4. C
5. B
6. A

Exercise 2
1. Let me
2. the place
3. Well
4. what I like
5. so
6. what I find

WRITING

Exercise 1
1. good
2. use your own style
3. short
4. an informal
5. Ask questions
6. Invite

Exercise 2
1. b
2. e
3. a
4. d
5. f
6. c

Exercise 3
a and d

UNIT 7

VOCABULARY

Exercise 1
1. style
2. suit
3. look
4. try
5. fit
6. afford

Exercise 2
1. loose
2. stripes
3. collar
4. buttons
5. sleeves
6. plain
7. pattern
8. tight

Exercise 3
1. untidy
2. display
3. goods
4. bargain
Shaded word: customers

Exercise 4

1 shoppers
2 messy
3 products
4 value
5 reductions
6 offers

Exercise 5

1 order
2 some
3 receipt
4 delivered
5 damaged
6 return
7 refund
8 exchange

GRAMMAR

Exercise 1

1 had bought
2 wore
3 couldn't afford
4 had seen

Exercise 2

1 they had spent all their
2 she had never been to
3 I could help him choose
4 I would lend her my
5 she loved my
6 he must get some

Exercise 3

1 told
2 said
3 tell
4 said
5 told
6 said

Exercise 4

1 where I was going; him (that) I was going
2 if/whether I liked her; (that) it looked
3 when he would start his; that he wasn't
4 if/whether I had found; her (that) I had found
5 what I had bought; (that) I had bought
6 if/whether she was going to ask for; (that) she had already done

LISTENING

Exercise 1

B

Exercise 2

A

Exercise 3

1 The plastic that is used to make them is plastic waste from the oceans.
2 It no longer uses plastic bags.
3 They stay in the ground for hundreds of years.
4 These clothes break down in the ground.
5 They can rent them cheaply.
6 They don't contain any animal products.
7 Because they are too expensive for her.

PUSH YOURSELF B2

2 advised me to use
3 warned me not to get
4 promised to exchange
5 told me to keep
6 invited me to

READING PART 1

1 A
2 B
3 C
4 B
5 A

SPEAKING

Exercise 1

1 would
2 Same
3 neither
4 mean
5 Do
6 too

Exercise 2

1 C
2 B
3 C
4 A
5 B
6 C

WRITING

Exercise 1

1 c
2 e
3 a
4 g
5 b
6 d
7 f

Exercise 2

1 P
2 N
3 N
4 P
5 P
6 N

Exercise 3

1 Although
2 and
3 though
4 but
5 as well

Exercise 4

1 selection
2 reasonable
3 like most
4 complaint
5 but
6 worth
7 recommend

UNIT 8
VOCABULARY

Exercise 1

1 cave
2 shore
3 waves
4 cliff
5 stones
6 leaves
7 riverbank
8 rainforest

Exercise 2

1 branches
2 sand dunes
3 waterfall
4 bushes
5 glacier
6 iceberg

Exercise 3

1 quiet
2 dense
3 empty
4 dry
5 noisy
6 humid

Exercise 4

1 grasslands
2 tropical forests
3 temperate forests
4 polar regions
1 B
2 C
3 D
4 A

Exercise 5

1 penguin
2 kangaroo
3 hedgehog
4 giraffe
5 polar bear
6 red squirrel
7 orangutan
8 red deer
9 arctic wolf
10 green iguana

Exercise 6

1 challenging
2 disappointed
3 amazing
4 exciting
5 worried
6 relaxing
7 surprised

GRAMMAR

Exercise 1

1 could
2 may not
3 must
4 can't
5 may
6 might
7 can't

Exercise 2

1 can't be scared
2 may go
3 might not see
4 could be
5 may not be
6 must be difficult

PUSH YOURSELF B2

1 tails; antlers
2 trunks; tusks
3 manes; hooves
4 paws; claws
5 feathers; beak

READING

Exercise 1

A 3
B 2
C 5
D 1

Exercise 2

1 true
2 false
3 false
4 false
5 true
6 false

LISTENING PART 4

1 A
2 C
3 C
4 B
5 C
6 B

SPEAKING

1 This is
2 There's
3 on
4 middle; can see
5 must be
6 sure
7 might
8 background

WRITING

Exercise 1

1 relaxing
2 clear
3 long
4 high
5 fresh
6 rocky

Exercise 2

1 and
2 Although
3 so
4 as well as
5 because
6 What's more

UNIT 9

VOCABULARY

Exercise 1

1 attend
2 education
3 qualifications
4 grades
5 skills
6 rules

Exercise 2

1 topic; lecture
2 pass; term
3 graduate; degree
4 revise; fail

Exercise 3

1 take
2 do
3 Pay
4 do
5 make
6 take
7 get

GRAMMAR

Exercise 1

1 are
2 was
3 were
4 is
5 are
6 isn't

Exercise 2

1 were sent
2 was opened by
3 is spent
4 aren't sold
5 weren't told
6 was caused by

Exercise 3

1 is encouraged
2 was stolen
3 are sent
4 were told
5 wasn't invited
6 isn't included

READING PART 3

1	C	4	A
2	D	5	D
3	C		

PUSH YOURSELF B2

1 has been broken
2 is being repaired
3 had been announced
4 should be cleaned
5 must be completed
6 can't be used

LISTENING

Exercise 1

C

Exercise 2

1 true
2 false
3 false
4 true
5 false
6 false

SPEAKING

Exercise 1

1 c
2 f
3 a
4 e
5 b
6 d

Exercise 2

1 don't
2 at
3 find
4 by
5 can't
6 thought

WRITING

Exercise 1

1 Dear
2 enquire
3 could
4 know
5 Finally
6 let
7 look
8 sincerely

Exercise 2

1 like to know where the course takes
2 you tell me if food is included in
3 let me know what I should
4 you tell me if I can get to
5 like to know if there is
6 let me know if the course is

UNIT 10

VOCABULARY

Exercise 1

1 port
2 ferry
3 traffic jam
4 flight
5 platform
6 delay
7 petrol station
Mystery word: boarding pass

Exercise 2

1 business class
2 airline
3 check-in
4 departure lounge
5 gate
6 cabin staff
7 flight attendant
8 cockpit

Exercise 3

1 got into
2 got out of
3 got off
4 get around
5 got to
6 got back

GRAMMAR

Exercise 1

1 go; prefer
2 complains; is
3 feel; walk
4 save; use
5 buy; are

Exercise 2

1 'll get; walk
2 will we do; isn't
3 'll miss; leave
4 pay; 'll buy
5 'll go; are

Exercise 3

1 go to the beach unless it's
2 won't go to the concert if the tickets are
3 won't buy me a car unless
4 only get a taxi if there are no
5 buy any shoes unless I see
6 'll come to the party if I don't have / won't come to the party if I have

Exercise 4

1 walk; 's
2 'll call; are
3 see; 'll tell
4 gets; is
5 go; are
6 will you do; breaks down

Exercise 5

1 would be
2 stopped
3 used
4 would be
5 had to
6 would use
7 would cause
8 didn't have
9 would make
10 would have
11 would need
12 changed
13 would grow
14 would use

Exercise 6

1 had
2 is
3 have
4 eat
5 would use
6 'll (will) come
7 have
8 walked

READING

Exercise 1

B

Exercise 2

1 V
2 K
3 K
4 A
5 V
6 A

PUSH YOURSELF B2

1 B
2 C
3 A
4 B

LISTENING PART 2

1 B
2 C
3 C
4 A
5 A
6 B

SPEAKING

Exercise 1

1 A
2 B
3 B
4 B
5 A
6 B

Exercise 2

1 must be
2 might/may/could be
3 can't be
4 may/might not be

WRITING

Exercise 1

1 was sitting
2 came
3 replied
4 looked
5 had agreed
6 was thinking
7 rang
8 asked

Exercise 2

1 'Nice to meet you,' she said.
2 'Where are you going?' he asked.
3 'Go away!' she shouted.
4 'Come with me,' he whispered quietly.

Exercise 3

1 whispered
2 asked
3 told
4 shouted
5 called

UNIT 11

VOCABULARY

Exercise 1
1. terraced house
2. cosy
3. old-fashioned
4. suburbs
5. two-storey
6. brand new
7. convenient
8. block of flats
9. business district
10. top floor

Exercise 2
1. A
2. B
3. C
4. C
5. C
6. A
7. C
8. A

Exercise 3
1. cabinet
2. heating
3. rug
4. cushions
5. wardrobe
6. sink

GRAMMAR

Exercise 1
1. where
2. that
3. which
4. whose
5. who
6. when
7. who/that
8. that

Exercise 2
1. which we looked at
2. who owns our flat
3. who lives in London
4. which is near the city centre
5. which is annoying

Exercise 3
1. D
2. D
3. ND
4. ND
5. ND
You can use *that* in sentences 1 and 2.

Exercise 4
4, 5, 7

Exercise 5
1. which/that I use
2. which/that they are building in the business district are
3. , who is really sporty,
4. , (which is) where I live, is
5. , which is
6. that/who I have met are

Exercise 6
1. had our photo taken
2. get my phone fixed
3. you had your hair cut
4. have your shopping delivered
5. get your running style checked

LISTENING

Exercise 1
C

Exercise 2
1. Andy
2. Ewan
3. Daisy
4. Andy
5. Daisy
6. Ewan

READING PART 5
1. C
2. B
3. D
4. A
5. A
6. C

PUSH YOURSELF B2
1. stunning
2. residential
3. furnished
4. delightful
5. spacious
6. unique
7. luxurious
8. picturesque

SPEAKING

Exercise 1
1. c
2. d
3. a
4. f, b
5. b, f

Exercise 2
1. B
2. C
3. A
4. A
5. C
6. B

WRITING

Exercise 1
1. for
2. on
3. afraid
4. could
5. seeing
6. back

Exercise 2
1. Dear
2. getting
3. unfortunately
4. Perhaps
5. looking
6. best

UNIT 12

VOCABULARY

Exercise 1
1. plumber
2. accountant
3. lawyer
4. pharmacist
5. electrician

Exercise 2
1. programmer
2. lecturer
3. politician
4. astronaut
5. architect

Exercise 3
1. patient
2. creative
3. intelligent
4. calm
5. friendly
6. reliable
7. organised
8. flexible

Exercise 4
1. co-workers
2. line manager
3. personal assistant
4. employee
5. sales staff
6. director
7. employer
8. freelancer

Exercise 5
1. certificate
2. good with
3. problem-solving
4. master's
5. doctorate
6. good at
7. communication

GRAMMAR

Exercise 1
1. Could
2. can
3. May
4. can't
5. Can
6. mustn't
7. Are we allowed to
8. can't

Exercise 2
1. had to be
2. weren't allowed to wear
3. had to wear
4. were allowed to keep

Exercise 3
1. B
2. A
3. B
4. B

Exercise 4
1. make me keep
2. don't let us use
3. wasn't allowed to go
4. had to go to bed
5. lets us look
6. 're not allowed to park

PUSH YOURSELF B2
1. must be able to see
2. will be able to talk
3. may/might be able to buy
4. should be able to camp
5. would be able to get

READING

Exercise 1
1. d
2. a
3. b
4. c

Exercise 2
1. E
2. D
3. A
4. B
5. C
6. F

Exercise 3
1. farmer
2. barista
3. tour guide
4. pharmacist
5. chef
6. childcare assistant

LISTENING PART 1
1. A
2. C
3. A
4. B
5. B
6. B
7. C

SPEAKING

Exercise 1
1. Sorry
2. Exactly
3. disagree
4. I'd

Exercise 2
1. Yes, you're right.
2. I don't think that's true.
3. I'm afraid I disagree.
4. I'd agree with that.

WRITING
1. opportunity
2. full-time
3. Applicants
4. should be able
5. must
6. qualifications
7. application

UNIT 13

VOCABULARY

Exercise 1

1 take up
2 joined
3 represent
4 take part
5 going out
6 beat
7 support
8 held
9 scored

Exercise 2

1 competitor
2 opponents
3 supporters
4 teammates
5 spectator
6 referee

Exercise 3

1	go	5	do
2	do	6	play
3	go	7	do
4	play		

Exercise 4

1	rink	5	course
2	pitch	6	track
3	pool	7	ramp
4	court		

GRAMMAR

Exercise 1

1 Climbing
2 spending
3 joining
4 practising
5 running
6 diving
7 buying
8 meeting

Exercise 2

1 's important to do
2 learnt to swim
3 can't wait to take part
4 wants to try
5 managed to win
6 's nice to meet
7 persuaded me to go
8 do yoga to relax
9 invited me to go
10 went into town to buy

Exercise 3

1 Spending
2 trying
3 to find
4 to have
5 to hire
6 buying
7 doing
8 to wear
9 wearing
10 to keep

LISTENING PART 3

1 August
2 cinema
3 painful
4 city
5 35/thirty-five minutes/mins
6 running

READING

Exercise 1

A

Exercise 2

1 false – He started two years after he moved to the coast.
2 true
3 false – He knew he had no choice but to stay with his surfboard and wait.
4 true
5 false – He was a little nervous about getting into the water again.

PUSH YOURSELF B2

1	up	5	got
2	at	6	out
3	have	7	get
4	pick	8	down

SPEAKING

Exercise 1

1 so
2 which is why
3 Because
4 since
5 As
6 because

Exercise 2

1	What's	6	that's
2	agree	7	How
3	should	8	Really
4	do	9	sure
5	right	10	don't

WRITING

Exercise 1

1 C
2 A
3 D

Exercise 2

1 also
2 because
3 both
4 which
5 too
6 but

Exercise 3

1 ~~there~~ their
2 ~~its~~ it's
3 ~~no~~ know
4 ~~hear~~ here
5 ~~quite~~ quiet
6 ~~by~~ buy

UNIT 14

VOCABULARY

Exercise 1

1 disappointed
2 shocked
3 nervous
4 miserable
5 depressed

Exercise 2

1 impressed
2 jealous
3 guilty
4 embarrassed
5 cheerful

Exercise 3

1 rude; cruel
2 stupid; generous
3 cute; curly
4 brave; patient

GRAMMAR

Exercise 1

1 loses
2 won't invite
3 would like
4 got
5 manage

Exercise 2

1 where she was going
2 was going
3 if he had finished his project
4 wanted to finish it
5 Emma had left the party
6 didn't know
7 if Tom was OK
8 wasn't; would talk

Exercise 3

1 who help you.
2 where she grew up.
3 whose dad is a chef
4 which we stayed in was huge.
5 which I was delighted

Exercise 4

1 can't
2 ought
3 should
4 able
5 must
6 don't have to
7 might
8 let
9 have
10 need to

READING

1	A	4	B
2	B	5	A
3	B	6	B

PUSH YOURSELF B2

1 blue-eyed
2 highly respected
3 well-paid
4 open-minded
5 long-haired
6 highly recommended

LISTENING PART 4

1 B
2 C
3 B
4 A
5 C
6 A

SPEAKING

Exercise 1

1 How
2 Can
3 often
4 Do
5 long
6 Is
7 Why
8 Which

Exercise 2

1	A	5	B
2	B	6	A
3	B	7	A
4	A	8	B

WRITING

Exercise 1

1 D, H
2 C, F
3 A, G
4 B, E

Exercise 2

1 but
2 so
3 Although
4 also
5 However
6 when
7 or
8 because

AUDIOSCRIPT

STARTER

🔊 Track 02

Narrator: 1 – Maria

Maria: I love my job! I'm really interested in food, and I love cooking. I also like reading old cookery books and learning new ways to prepare food. But I don't want to work as a chef in a restaurant because you have to work at night – I like hanging out with my friends in the evenings! I usually have breakfast at eight o'clock and then start work. I start preparing a meal, then I get the video camera and start filming. A lot of people watch my shows online, which is great, and I'm starting to earn some money from them too. When I've got enough money, I want to visit different countries and learn different cooking skills, so I can use them in my vlogs.

Narrator: 2 – Sam

Sam: I enjoy lots of different sports, but tennis is my favourite. My parents are always saying to me, 'Why don't you become a sports teacher?' But I don't want to teach other people – I want to play myself! I'm winning quite a lot of games at the moment, so I really hope I can become a professional player. I'd love to see a photograph of myself in the newspaper one day, and read a report about one of my games! I have to watch what I eat, so I don't go to restaurants very often – pizzas aren't very good if you're serious about sport! I also listen to music a lot at home, and I sometimes go to concerts.

Narrator: 3 – Anika

Anika: My life is busy at the moment. I go to college three days a week, and I also work for a newspaper in my town. Not much happens in my town – there isn't much crime, so the police don't have much to do! But there are sometimes big sports events or music events. I enjoy writing reports about those. I think writing is my talent, so this is the right job for me. When I'm working, I always arrive at the office early, and they tell me which story to report. I talk to lots of different people for my job, which I enjoy. One day I might interview a doctor, then the next day I might talk to customers in a supermarket. Every day is different, which is great!

🔊 Track 03

1   I'm really interested in food.
2   I don't want to work as a chef in a restaurant.
3   I'm winning quite a lot of games at the moment.
4   I also listen to music a lot at home.
5   I also work for a newspaper in my town.
6   This is the right job for me.

UNIT 1

🔊 Track 04

Terry: Hi, and welcome to The Holiday Show. I'm Terry Maynard.

Lisa: And I'm Lisa Brighty.

Terry: Now, we're always looking for unusual holiday stories. Lisa, what have you found this week?

Lisa: Well, this is the story about the holiday company *Top Cruises*. As you know, a cruise is a luxury holiday on board a ship that travels around and visits different places. This company is now offering someone the chance to work as a professional tourist on their cruises!

Terry: So, you mean, they get paid to go on holiday?

Lisa: Exactly! The company runs seven different cruises during the summer, and they want someone to go on four of these cruises for them.

Terry: And what do they have to do? What's the 'job' part of it? Do they have to entertain the guests, or write a blog, something like that?

Lisa: No, they don't have to write anything. Believe it or not, all they have to do is post three photos a day on social media.

Terry: Really? That sounds like a really easy job! Can they be any kinds of photos?

Lisa: No. I thought it might be a bit boring, you know, just lots of photos of the ship to show how wonderful it is. But it has to be a mixture of scenery, people they meet and things they experience, either on the ship or when they visit places on the shore.

Terry: That doesn't sound like much work. Is there anything else?

Lisa: Yes. They have to make a short video to post on social media. This sounds a bit more difficult because the holiday company will choose a subject for them and they have to follow this.

Terry: That doesn't sound too bad. And what do they receive in return?

Lisa: They get all their travel expenses, of course, and all their food, and also spending money of about £1,000 a week, so they can buy things to remind them of their trip.

Terry: Wow! So, why is the company doing this?

Lisa: Well, it certainly isn't because their cruise ships are empty! They know that most people who want to go on a cruise look online for ideas. So they want to get lots of amazing photos of their cruises onto the internet, so that when people start searching, they'll find them and decide to book their own trip.

Terry: And how will they choose the right person for the job? Does it have to be someone who knows a lot about travel?

Lisa: No, they want someone who can take good photos and show that they've had an amazing time. So, if you want to apply, you don't send a letter – just email some examples of your own holiday posts. And you never know, you might just get this dream job. I think I might apply myself!

UNIT 2

🔊 Track 05

Narrator: For each question, choose the correct answer.
1 – You will hear two friends talking about a film they have just seen.

Man: So, did you enjoy that?

Woman: It was certainly different to the movies we normally go to. I enjoyed the special effects, but they were so noisy in places, it spoiled my enjoyment. I missed a lot of what the characters were saying to each other, so I didn't know what was going on. It was such a shame. I'm sure we've seen the leading actor in something else.

Man: Yeah, she was in that romantic comedy last month. You know, the one that felt like it went on for hours and hours.

Woman: Oh yes, I remember. That wasn't great either.

Narrator: Now listen again.

Narrator: 2 – You will hear a brother and sister talking about booking concert tickets.

Woman: I guess we need to book seats for the concert soon. Otherwise they'll be sold out.

Man: Well, here's the seating plan on the website. Lots of seats on the left- or right-hand sides of the hall.

Woman: Hardly surprising, you can't see properly unless you get seats in the centre. Look, there's a couple free in the middle of the fourth row. How fantastic!

Man: But look at the price! Let's see what's available in the balcony.

Woman: Mm, quite a few, but they're not much cheaper.

Man: OK. Then I think it's worth paying a bit more.

Woman: Absolutely.

Narrator: Now listen again.

Narrator: 3 – You will hear a woman telling a friend about a TV programme.

Woman: Tim, did you watch TV last night? There was a fantastic programme on.

Man: No, I was out.

Woman: Shame. It was filmed on a Scottish island – the one where they made your favourite police detective dramas – I can't remember the name of the programme – and it was about a group of people there and how they're trying to live without electricity, cars, and so on, and growing all their own food. And of course, the scenery was really dramatic.

Man: Sounds interesting. I'll try and watch it next week.

Woman: It was just a single show, but it's probably available online.

Narrator: Now listen again.

Narrator: 4 – You will hear two people talking about online newspapers.

Man: What are you reading?

Woman: An article on my favourite newspaper website. It's really good for news about sport.

Man: Yes, I always get my news online now. I mean, for people who haven't got much time or only want the basic facts, it's better to catch the news headlines on the television. I've noticed, though, that all news programmes and newspapers cover the same issues, but if you want full explanations and answers to the real questions, you have to *read* the news rather than listen to it.

Woman: Yes, that's probably true.

Narrator: Now listen again.

Narrator: 5 – You will hear a man telling a friend about a play called *The Visit*.

Man: I finally went to a performance of *The Visit* at the theatre last night. I was so looking forward to it. Eddy Smith is my favourite director and I've waited ages to go to another of his productions.

Woman: And what was it like?

Man: Different to his usual work, but it made me think a lot. And at least I can now join in conversations when people are discussing it.

Woman: Well, please don't tell me how it finishes because I'm going to see it next week.

Man: I won't say a word.

Narrator: Now listen again.

Narrator: 6 – You will hear two friends talking about a summer music festival.

Woman: I've got my ticket for this year's Fun in the Sun festival.

Man: You go every year, don't you?

Woman: Yeah, it's my favourite event of the summer. Since it started getting more popular, it costs loads more to get in. But then I don't have to pay to get there as it's only down the road from my parents' house. People who come from further away often get stuck in traffic for ages.

Man: Perhaps I'll get tickets this year too.

Woman: Great. We can arrange to meet somewhere there. Otherwise we'll never see each other among the hundreds of people.

Narrator: Now listen again.

Narrator: That is the end of Part 2.

UNIT 3

🔊 **Track 06**

Presenter: Hi and welcome to The Food Show. Today I'm talking to Elsa Brooks, a food journalist. Nice to have you here.

Elsa: It's great to be here.

Presenter: And you're going to tell us about a very different restaurant in New York. What's different about this restaurant, Elsa?

Elsa: Well, it's a normal restaurant in some ways – you order food from a waiter and pay your bill at the end. But the people who cook the food aren't professional chefs, so they have no training. They are all grandmothers – ordinary women who are used to cooking everyday food for their families, so the kind of food you eat there is the kind of delicious traditional food your own grandmother might cook for you.

🔊 **Track 07**

Presenter: So how did you first learn about this restaurant, Elsa?

Elsa: Well, as you know I read restaurant reviews all the time, and I'm always looking for new restaurants to try, but I didn't know about this one until a friend mentioned it to me, and I thought: I have to go there! You don't see many advertisements for it, so I'm really glad I found out about it.

Presenter: Now, the owner is called Mr Scaravella, I believe. Why did he want to start a restaurant with grandmothers for cooks?

Elsa: Well, clearly there are a lot of great restaurants in New York, and people eat out all the time and spend a lot of money on eating out. But actually Mr Scaravella started this restaurant because his own grandmother had died, and he had wonderful memories of eating her home-cooked food.

Presenter: So, what's the menu like?

Elsa: Well, Mr Scaravella is Italian, and half the menu is Italian food, cooked by Italian grandmothers – that doesn't change. Then the other half of the menu is cooked by a different grandmother every night, and they come from all over the world, and cook their own traditional dishes from their countries. And the people who go there to eat love *all* these different dishes!

Presenter: So, tell us about the different women who cook at the restaurant.

Elsa: Well, there's always a main cook for the night, and then a helper, usually someone from a different country. And the great thing is that because the food they cook is all so different, they don't compete with each other to try to be the best. They really enjoy trying the dishes the other women cook, and they learn little tips from each other, about new things they can try.

Presenter: And they also have cooking classes there, don't they?

Elsa: Yes. The classes are run by the grandmothers who cook there, and they're a chance for them to share their skills and their recipes. The classes are all female. They aren't too expensive, but they are very popular, so you need to book well in advance.

Presenter: And finally, how was your experience of eating in the restaurant?

Elsa: Oh, it was amazing! There was a great atmosphere, and everyone was really friendly – the waiters, especially. I managed to talk to some of the other guests too, which was nice. But the food was the best bit. It was amazing – really good, home-cooked dishes. The cook was Japanese the evening I was there, and I'll definitely go back and hopefully try a dish from a different country!

UNIT 4

🎧 Track 08

Narrator: For each question, choose the correct answer.
1 – Where will the woman go camping this summer?

Man: Are you camping again this summer?

Woman: Yes, but we're trying somewhere new. We've camped at the same place up in the mountains for the last three years, and it's been great going for walks in the forest. But that site's closed now, so we're staying on a farm.

Man: That sounds really peaceful.

Woman: Oh, I imagine the animals will wake us up really early. It was either camp in the field, or by the river, and I thought the sound of water would keep me awake all night.

Narrator: Now listen again.

Narrator: 2 – What's the view from the apartment block?

Man: Hi, Pete. I've just arrived at my holiday apartment. It's right in the city centre, in what must be the tallest building around. There are windows on two sides and they're huge. Across the square I can see an enormous statue of someone – I'm not sure who, but I'll go down and look later. I want to find out about taxis too because there's a famous bridge somewhere in this part of town that I want to go across. I'll send you some photos.

Narrator: Now listen again.

Narrator: 3 – Which activity did the woman help with?

Man: How was your weekend?

Woman: Great, but I'm exhausted now. I've become a volunteer for a charity that looks after the countryside. You know, doing things like cutting down plants that are growing in the wrong place and making it difficult for walkers to use the paths. I spent all weekend clearing rubbish out of streams and I'm going back next weekend as they need volunteers to rebuild some of the old field walls.

Narrator: Now listen again.

Narrator: 4 – Where will the friends meet before going to the theatre?

Woman: Will you have enough time to meet and go for a pizza before we go to the theatre tomorrow evening?

Man: Probably not. My last lecture doesn't finish till six-fifteen.

Woman: Well, I if you're coming straight from the university, I'll wait for you by the art gallery.

Man: OK, I should be there around 7.

Woman: I think I'll go shopping before I meet you. And I can get a takeaway pizza in the shopping centre.

Man: OK. See you at 7 then.

Narrator: Now listen again.

Narrator: 5 – Where is the problem in the apartment building?

Woman: So this is your apartment building. The entrance is very modern, and the automatic doors make it look really smart.

Man: Yes, I don't know how I'd get in if they stopped working. I think there's probably someone to call if I have any problems. Actually, I need to do that already because when you come out of the lift, it's really dark in the hall outside my flat. The light bulb needs changing.

Woman: Well, do you want to phone someone before we go in?

Man: I will, if you don't mind waiting.

Narrator: Now listen again.

Narrator: 6 – What did the woman do in the park?

Woman: Hi, Natalie. I'm phoning because I was in the park this morning – I'd gone there to do some reading but the seats by the fountain were gone because they were doing some repairs to it. Anyway, I'd just finished taking pictures of these beautiful flowers and as I stood up, a jogger ran past me. You won't believe it, but I've just realised that it was Daniel from school. He must be back from Australia. Do you still have his number?

Narrator: Now listen again.

Narrator: 7 – Where in the city will they eat tonight?

Man: Do you mind where we go for a meal this evening?

Woman: I'd rather not go to a fast food place. I hate the long queues there and anyway I'd prefer something a bit healthier than burgers and fries. There's a food truck by the river that sells sushi. It shouldn't be too busy, and it's certainly cheaper than eating in a restaurant.

Man: Sounds good to me. I'm not exactly dressed for anywhere really smart.

Woman: Me neither. And also it's a lovely place to go for a walk afterwards.

Narrator: Now listen again.

Narrator: That is the end of Part 1.

UNIT 5

 Track 09

Elly: Hi, I'm Elly Barlow, and today we're talking about fitness. Now, I'm not as fit as I should be, and I hate the gym! But there are lots of apps that promise to get you fit in just a few minutes each day. Is that possible? With me is Jake Milburn, a personal trainer. He's tried four apps for us. What did you find, Jake?

Jake: Well, the first one I chose is 'Ten-minute Yoga'. Each day it gives you a new workout with ten different exercises, which take one minute each. The idea is to make your body stronger and able to move more easily. You have to hold each position for as long as possible, for a minute if you can. One problem is that there's no voice, so you have to read the instructions. That's difficult while you're doing the exercises.

Elly: Will it get me fit?

Jake: No, you need to work harder than this to get fit.

Elly: OK. What's next?

Jake: 'Daily Fit Club' has 12-minute workouts to make your heart and muscles stronger. The exercises are quite difficult, and they'll definitely make your heart work. One problem is that the exercises have strange names like 'tuck jumps' and 'air jacks'. The instructor just calls out these names, so you need to learn all the names before you try the workouts. Also, you have to be quite fit before you start, so it isn't really suitable for beginners.

Elly: No good for me, then.

Jake: Probably not. The next one is 'Burn the Fat'. This has 10-minute workouts that aim to burn body fat and make you thinner and fitter. The workouts aren't easy, and they feel much longer than 10 minutes. I'm pretty fit, and I got hot and out of breath! The exercises are good, but they're not very interesting and you repeat them lots of times. I think most people would lose interest and give up on this one!

Elly: Definitely no good for me, then. What about the last one?

Jake: This was 'Superfit in Ten'. I loved this. It's for beginners, and it uses videos to show you what to do, so it's clear and easy to follow. The exercises start easy and get harder as you do more workouts. The workouts are fun, they'll definitely get your heart beating fast, and your muscles will get stronger.

Elly: It sounds like a good one for me.

Jake: Yeah, it's a great app for you, and will definitely get you fitter, but only if you use it every day!

Elly: Thanks, Jake.

UNIT 6

 Track 10

Narrator: For each question, write the correct answer in the gap. Write one or two words or a number or a date or a time. You have twenty seconds to look at Part 3.

Narrator: You will hear a journalist called Steffi talking about a week she spent without using social media.

Steffi: I'm Steffi and I'd like to tell you about something I did recently – I gave up social media for a whole week.

When I was at school, I was too busy with activities at home to use social media. I saw my friends every day anyway. Then, when I went to university, I wanted to keep in contact with people back home, so that's when I first went on social media.

Mostly I used social media for reading friends' messages. Instead of writing long replies, I put selfies on my social media page. People could see where I was and how much fun I was having.

When I started working, I noticed I was using social media loads more. It was probably only 10 minutes at a time. But in a day, it was more than two hours. I decided to write an article about social media. I interviewed people, and some said they used social media for three hours a day.

Anyway, last week I stopped going on social media completely. I knew I needed something else to read, and I'm not a big fan of reading magazines, so I chose a novel. And I really enjoyed it.

At the beginning of the week, I expected to feel worried about not knowing what friends were doing. But I had more time to call people, and I met some friends after work, which was lovely. At the end of seven days, I definitely wasn't as stressed, even though it was really busy at work.

So, will I change my social media habits? Well, I've deleted almost all social media apps from my phone. I'm going to check the news app, but only in the evening for no more than twenty minutes. And I definitely plan to see friends more.

Narrator: Now listen again.

Narrator: That is the end of Part 3.

UNIT 7

 Track 11

Kiera: Hi. Welcome to The World of Clothes. I'm Kiera Samson, and this is my weekly podcast on everything to do with clothes and fashion. And usually I'm talking about things like where to find clothes that look good, or clothes that are good value and not too expensive to buy. But this week I want to talk about something a bit different – ethical clothes – that means, clothes that are made in a good way – a way that doesn't harm the planet, so they don't cause pollution, and they treat people well too, by paying fair wages and giving people good working conditions.

 Track 12

Kiera: So, I've been looking at ethical clothes online, and there are some great ideas out there. For example, there's a really stylish pair of blue trainers here. What's special about them? Well, we all know that there's a huge amount of waste plastic in the ocean, and it's damaging marine animals. So now one company is using this plastic waste to make trainers. You can get them in different colours and I must say they look pretty trendy. The company that makes them is making a real effort to help the environment. For example, last year they completely stopped using plastic bags in their shops – they only use paper ones now, and that's got to be a good thing!

Now, if trainers aren't your thing, maybe food is. Food and clothes, you're asking – what's that about? Well, a company in Sweden that makes outdoor clothes is trying to deal with the problem of all the clothes we throw away. As you know, a lot of the rubbish we throw away is buried in the ground, and most modern clothes stay there for hundreds of years. But this company's clothes are all made from completely natural materials, so when they go into the ground as rubbish, they break down, and you can even grow vegetables in the waste they produce. Cool, eh? Their clothes are expensive, of course, and a lot of people can't afford to buy them, but another good thing about them is that they allow you to *rent* them cheaply, and you can give them back when you've finished using them!

Another website that I found is called GoodClothes.com, and this sells all kinds of clothes that are made in an ethical way. There are different signs next to the clothes that tell you what's good about each item. For example, a lot of their clothes are made without any animal products, so they're perfect if you're a vegetarian, or you care about animals. Other signs show that the people who make the clothes get a fair wage for their work, or the clothes are made with local materials. There are some really cool T-shirts on there, and I'd love to buy one, but I'm afraid they're just too expensive for me.

So, that's it for this week. I hope I've given you some things to think about. Bye for now, and happy shopping!

UNIT 8

🔊 Track 13

Narrator: For each question, choose the correct answer. You have 45 seconds to look at the questions for Part 4.

Presenter: I'm talking to Rob Tucker, a wildlife expert who's studied camels in Australia. Rob, how did you get interested in camels?

Rob: I've been interested in all animals that were introduced into Australia by Europeans – camels, buffaloes, rabbits, horses and sheep of course – for quite a long time. When I was a student, a movie came out about a woman called Robyn Davidson who crossed an Australian desert with four camels. I actually missed it but someone gave me a book she'd written about her adventure – I really enjoyed it and it made me want to learn more about these amazing creatures.

Presenter: When did camels arrive in Australia?

Rob: One was brought here in 1840. Then, in the 1860s, many more arrived on ships. To start with, they came with camel farmers who knew how to handle and train them. Camel farms were set up and soon there were thousands of camels – the perfect animal to help explorers discover Australia. Camels born on the farms worked harder and carried more than the original camels. I should mention those camels were mostly from India. It's easy to forget camels aren't just from Arabian countries.

Presenter: Why were camels so useful? I know they don't need water every day.

Rob: Well, there's water even in the desert. For me, camels had the advantages of horses – they could carry people and equipment over rough countryside – but they had the added benefit of keeping going all day, stopping to rest only at night.

Presenter: Not all Australians today like camels, do they?

Rob: No. Most camels today are wild. There's hundreds of thousands of them – and that's a problem for sheep and cow farmers. Some parts of Australia haven't had rain for several years. Camels go onto farms and dig holes to get to pipes carrying water to farmhouses and to where sheep and cows go to drink. So farmers are always having to do repairs.

Presenter: Camels are also a tourist attraction, aren't they?

Rob: Yeah … if you haven't tried a camel ride, you should. It's amazing to ride into the desert and camp under the stars for two nights, returning only at the end of the third day. Obviously, if visitors don't have much time, they go for a day, or even take half-day trips, but I don't think that's enough.

Presenter: How easy is it to see camels in the wild?

Rob: Surprisingly difficult, especially if you're driving along the road, even though their numbers are still growing. The thing is, they're more or less the same brown as the countryside. This makes them very easy to miss, especially if they're not moving.

Presenter: Of course …

Narrator: Now listen again.

Narrator: That is the end of Part 4.

UNIT 9

🔊 Track 14

Presenter: Welcome to the show. Today we're talking about learning as an adult, and with me is Stella Bradshaw. Her book, *Never too late to learn*, was published last month. Stella, why did you write the book?

Stella: Well, I first went to university when I was 26. I wasn't a 'good student' at school, and for me it was a great achievement to finally get my degree. It made me realise that learning isn't just for school. It's something you can do all your life. I wanted to encourage other people to keep learning!

Presenter: Is it difficult to study as an adult?

Stella: No. Colleges and universities welcome older students. Last year a degree was awarded to Mavis Bowman, who's 86! She left school at 15, mainly because her parents needed her to work to help pay the bills. She was never really interested in learning, and it was only when her grandson asked her for help with a project that she realised what a pleasure learning was, and decided to get a degree.

Presenter: That's amazing! Is it harder to learn when you're older?

Stella: It can be slightly more difficult to remember things, like facts, but this doesn't mean that older people learn more slowly. In general they work harder than younger people, so they learn just as fast – remember, they're learning because they want to, not because they have to.

Presenter: Now, the book also deals with other kinds of learning, like learning a language, art, music, or sport. Why do you think it's so important to keep learning?

Stella: Learning something new helps you feel more confident – can you remember that amazing feeling you had as a child when you managed to do something new for the first time? But most of all, it stops life from getting boring!

Presenter: You interviewed a lot of people for the book, and there are some great stories. What's your favourite?

Stella: I think that's Kevin Jones, who learned to ride a bike at the age of 28. He describes how difficult it was and what the experience taught him, like it's OK to admit you can't do something, and you shouldn't judge other people, and, most importantly, sometimes there are no quick solutions and you have to keep trying if you want to succeed.

Presenter: Finally, what's your advice for our listeners?

Stella: Never think that something is too difficult for you. If you couldn't do it in the past, it doesn't mean you can't do it now. So if you want to play a musical instrument or take up a sport, learn a language, or get a degree: just do it!

UNIT 10

🔊 Track 15

Narrator: 1.

Woman: I ride my bike everywhere, and I think these new cycle paths are great. It's dangerous to ride on the main roads because most car drivers don't pay attention to bikes. Having proper cycle paths is much better. I like the fact that there are lights, too, which means you can use them even when it's dark, and you know you aren't in any danger.

Narrator: 2.

Man: I've tried using the new cycle paths, because it would be great for me if I could get to work by bike every day. They're OK, and I guess I'll get used to them. But I think they need to put some signs up to help people see which way to go, especially through the park. It isn't always clear at the moment.

Narrator: 3.

Woman: Well, it's good to see that the city is trying to do more to encourage people to use their bikes. But I really don't think they've done very well with these. They're too narrow, which means they're difficult to use when there are a lot of bikes, and they don't go to places where anyone wants to go. To be honest, I think they're a complete waste of time!

Narrator: 4.

Man: I've used them quite a lot. There are plenty of them, and there's one that goes very close to the place where I work. It's great to be able to avoid the main roads, but in a way, I think they've been too successful. There are so many bikes on them in the mornings that it almost feels as if you're riding on a busy road!

🅐 **Track 16**

Narrator: For each question, choose the correct answer.
1 – You will hear two friends talking about a new airport.

Man: Wow, this is an amazing airport! How long has it been open?

Woman: Only about two or three months. I love the design of the building, although I thought we were going to get lost when we were driving in.

Man: Yes, the information was quite confusing. But they've clearly put a lot of thought into collecting rubbish – with separate bins for plastic, paper, food, and so on.

Woman: And you don't have to look around to find them. It's just a shame the airport's on the opposite side of the city to where we live.

Man: At least we don't hear any noise.

Narrator: Now listen again.

Narrator: 2 – You will hear a woman telling her brother about her new electric bicycle.

Woman: I rode my new electric bike to college today.

Man: And?

Woman: Well, people who don't know me don't know that I have to cycle up those really steep hills near our house. And it's really flat around college. So I felt a bit uncomfortable – I mean it makes me look lazy. I'm sure people were looking at me as I parked it with the other bikes.

Man: I wouldn't worry about that.

Woman: I can't help it. Still, the bike's great quality. If I look after it, I should be able keep it for years.

Narrator: Now listen again.

Narrator: 3 – You will hear two colleagues talking about travelling to work.

Woman: There must be something happening in town today. Do you know, it took me 15 minutes to find a parking space this morning! Do you still catch the train to work?

Man: Yes. I'd never go back to driving. Sitting in traffic at the end of the day used to make me so cross.

Woman: I guess it must be useful to be able to send emails and read reports on the train before you even get to work.

Man: I only read for pleasure in the mornings.

Narrator: Now listen again.

Narrator: 4 – You will hear two friends talking about getting to the airport.

Man: Julia, about going to the airport next week … Last time we arranged to meet by the entrance it took us ages to find each other.

Woman: Yes, there was a huge tour group there. So why don't I come to your house?

Man: I can't make you do that. It would mean a very long journey for you. I was going to say, maybe we should look at the airport plan and find a better place to meet – like by the bus station, or the pick-up point.

Woman: Yes. Let's check online now.

Narrator: Now listen again.

Narrator: 5 – You will hear two neighbours talking about traffic in the town.

Woman: I'm so glad the roadworks are finished now. The traffic jams were awful.

Man: Hmm, there was someone on the radio saying wider roads simply encourage more traffic. The issue for me is that local people will get used to the new one-way system, but if you don't know the town, it's so easy to get lost now.

Woman: And you can't just turn around.

Man: Well, it's too late to change it now.

Woman: Perhaps they should build a huge car park on the edge of town.

Man: They talked about doing that once before, but the shop owners were against it.

Narrator: Now listen again.

Narrator: 6 – You will hear two friends talking about recycling.

Woman: Tom, is that a new water bottle?

Man: Yes, it's made of metal. It means I don't have to buy plastic bottles of water when I'm out.

Woman: I might get one of those. I've already got a cup made of bamboo, for when I'm out and want to get a coffee. Plastic's such a big problem, isn't it? I mean, some things I buy at the shop only come in bottles made of plastic. And I've almost given up buying things in jars because glass isn't environmentally friendly to produce.

Man: Oh, I know. It's impossible to know what to do sometimes.

Narrator: Now listen again.

Narrator: That is the end of Part 2.

UNIT 11

🅐 **Track 17**

Presenter: Welcome to the show. Living in London isn't easy, but with me today are three young people who are happy with how they've chosen to live in the capital. First, Ewan, a designer. Where do you live?

Ewan: I live in an empty office block. People often think it's against the law, but I rent through an agency. The owners prefer to have people living there, to keep the building safe until a business moves in. The advantage is that the rent is really cheap, and I don't have to travel far to work. The disadvantage is there's only one office toilet for 12 people on my floor, and the only shower is one we've set up ourselves. Also, I might have to move out at any time if a business wants to move in. But it's worth it because I can save money to get my own place.

Presenter: That's really interesting. Now Daisy, a nurse, has found a different way to live. Tell us where you live, Daisy.

Daisy: I live with an 89-year-old lady, Julie, in her house. Lots of elderly people live alone in London, and they're often lonely. Sharing the house with a young person is a good solution – cheap rent in return for friendship. So, from Monday to Friday, I cook with Julie in the evenings, or we go out for a meal. Actually, she's great fun, and she's given me lots of useful advice about all kinds of things. The disadvantages? It was difficult at first because I wasn't used to living with someone older, but it's fine now. And I've saved lots of money! I'm moving out soon, into my own flat, but Julie and I have become friends, so I'll still see her.

Presenter: What a lovely story. And finally, Andy, a musician. Tell us about your home.

Andy: I live on a boat on the river. I bought it last year, and I love it! The main advantages are that it's cheap and it's my own, so I can decorate it or do whatever I want with it. The disadvantages are that I have to look after it and do repairs, and emptying the toilet every week isn't much fun! It wouldn't suit someone who likes to live somewhere comfortable! The other problem is that I have to move around. You're only allowed to stay in one place for 14 days, then you have to move. But, on the positive side, I've made lots of friends with other young people who are doing the same thing as me – that's really nice.

UNIT 12

🌀 Track 18

Narrator: For each question, choose the correct answer.

1 – What is the woman's job now?

Woman: I'm really interested in buildings and their history. For a few years, I taught on a local history course at the university in my city. I really enjoyed sharing my knowledge with students but I didn't enjoy being indoors every day. Now I share what I know with visitors to the city by leading walking tours around all the important buildings – old and new – in the city centre.

Narrator: Now listen again.

Narrator: 2 – Which benefit does the man's company offer staff?

Woman: Are you glad you moved to a new company?

Man: Absolutely. It's a great firm to work for. There's a free car park for staff, which has made my journey to work a lot easier. And another thing they provide is free health checks twice a year. I've got my first one next month, so I've decided to join a gym – I don't want to be told I'm unfit.

Woman: What a good idea.

Narrator: Now listen again.

Narrator: 3 – Who works in the sales department?

Woman: I work in the sales department of a small company that makes equipment for hospitals. My manager's called Anna, and I get on really well with her. There used to be two men as well, but one of them left. That's made things really busy recently, but we're supposed to be getting another member of staff soon. My friend Sally has applied for the job but she hasn't heard yet if she's got an interview.

Narrator: Now listen again.

Narrator: 4 – Where does the man work?

Woman: Are you still working at the art gallery?

Man: No, that was just a part-time job while I was looking for something more permanent. There's a shopping centre that's opening next week behind the art gallery, and they've hired me to be head of security.

Woman: That's great. When do you start?

Man: Actually, I already have. It's great – it's the same journey time as the gallery, and when the centre opens, I'll be able to have lunch in a different restaurant every day.

Woman: Perhaps we could meet for lunch one day.

Man: Sure.

Narrator: Now listen again.

Narrator: 5 – What does the woman like best about her job?

Man: How are you getting on at work?

Woman: Fine. I've been promoted. I'm now personal assistant to the accountant. I don't have my own office but that's OK because the people I share an office with are quite nice. And the company recently installed this *amazing* new accounts software. It makes going to work every day a pleasure.

Man: The views must be great – I mean, isn't your office on the top floor?

Woman: Yes, you can see right across the city. To be honest, I rarely have time for looking out the window.

Narrator: Now listen again.

Narrator: 6 – What was the man's career ambition when he was a child?

Man: When I was a kid, I dreamed of running away from school and getting a boat and sailing round the world. I also used to race round the garden being a train driver, telling everyone that's what I was going to be when I grew up. When I was eight, I remember my parents taking me on a helicopter ride – I loved the speed and the sense of feeling free. I still get that feeling in my job as a pilot, especially when I look out of the plane at the ground below.

Narrator: Now listen again.

Narrator: 7 – Who is the woman's sister?

Man: What's your sister doing now she's left college? She wanted to work in television, didn't she?

Woman: Oh, she's opened her own café!

Man: I bet the food's delicious. She was always a great cook.

Woman: Well actually she's got a couple of people who run the kitchen. It means she has time to work out front, chatting to customers about what they like.

Man: I can see her being brilliant at that. She's confident and she has good people skills.

Narrator: Now listen again.

Narrator: That is the end of Part 1.

UNIT 13

Track 19

Narrator: For each question, write the correct answer in the gap. Write one or two words or a number or a date or a time. You have twenty seconds to look at Part 3.

Narrator: You will hear a gym owner called Lee Norton talking about a spin class.

Lee: I'm Lee Norton from Norton's Gym. I'd like to tell you about a class we're offering – a spin class with virtual reality. I hope you'll decide to join.

For those of you who haven't heard of spinning, it's indoor cycling on a machine, and it gives you a great workout. We've offered ordinary spin classes since January, when the gym opened. I did a spin class with virtual reality when I visited New York in May – I loved it and had to have it in my gym. Finally, in August, we were ready to open the class.

If you haven't done spin with virtual reality, it's like a spin class but in the dark, and you watch a huge screen as you cycle. I describe it as a way to enjoy fitness *and* cinema – it's not often you can do those two things together.

Spin with virtual reality is a fantastic workout. People who've tried it said it wasn't as boring as regular exercise because they had something else to think about. I personally thought it made the whole thing less painful, and the time went more quickly than in a traditional class.

So what do you watch while you're doing the spin class? We have several 'programmes' and I've tried them all. We change these regularly to keep it interesting. One week there's a ride through the countryside, or the city – my personal favourite – or on a race track.

If you're new to spin classes, I'd suggest the level one class, which lasts thirty-five minutes. It's best to arrive fifteen minutes early for the first session, so you can meet the instructor. You'll soon be ready to manage the next level, which is forty-five minutes long.

Customers tell me how much they like the virtual reality classes, so I'm intending to offer a wider choice of virtual reality fitness activities than just cycling, starting with running. And if that's popular, we might consider rowing classes.

Narrator: Now listen again.

Narrator: That is the end of Part 3.

UNIT 14

Track 20

Narrator: For each question, choose the correct answer. You have 45 seconds to look at the questions for Part 4.

Narrator: You will hear an interview with a musician called Molly Ford, talking about growing up with famous parents.

Presenter: My guest today is singer-songwriter Molly Ford. Welcome, Molly.

Molly: Thank you.

Presenter: Your parents are successful musicians too. When you were growing up, at what point did you realise they were famous?

Molly: All through my childhood, people came up to chat to them in the street. I just thought everyone was being friendly. Once, at a friend's house, there was a music magazine on the table. Mum and Dad were on the cover. I thought 'wow, they must be real stars'. I don't remember photographers following them. Maybe I didn't notice.

Presenter: What was it like touring with your parents?

Molly: An adventure. No two days were the same, you never felt stuck in a routine. I had mates, because the other musicians in the band took their families too. Sometimes staying in hotels was annoying. I wanted to sleep in my own bed and have my things around me. I hated leaving my toys behind when I was little.

Presenter: Did you ever read stuff about your parents when you were growing up?

Molly: My parents gave lots of interviews and were always open. I don't remember them ever getting cross because of lies about them in the newspapers. They were very proud of me, and still are – and it was kind of lovely to see things they'd said about me.

Presenter: Have your parents given you advice about being famous?

Molly: When I was a teenager, I got embarrassed if classmates kept asking me questions about them. Mum and Dad encouraged me to see the positive sides of being famous – the money, the chances to meet celebrities, and so on. Apart from that, we didn't talk about it. We were a happy family. Living out of suitcases was a temporary thing, but it was normal to us.

Presenter: I imagine your parents had famous friends.

Molly: Yes – I still see them now. They're interested in my career, and are great at listening to me if I have problems. It makes me laugh when I see them doing ordinary things, like washing up – I can't help thinking 'you're a worldwide superstar'. When I watch them on TV, I notice they don't behave the same as at home – they're more careful in what they say and do.

Presenter: Interesting. If you have children one day, will you take them on tour?

Molly: I don't know. I love working in the music industry, but travelling's tiring. Most probably I'd move into music producing or write songs for other people. I'd like to think my parents could be babysitters, but they'll probably still be touring!

Presenter: And what…

Narrator: Now listen again.

Narrator: That is the end of Part 4.

ACKNOWLEDGEMENTS

The authors and publishers acknowledge the following sources of copyright material and are grateful for the permissions granted. While every effort has been made, it has not always been possible to identify the sources of all the material used, or to trace all copyright holders. If any omissions are brought to our notice, we will be happy to include the appropriate acknowledgements on reprinting and in the next update to the digital edition, as applicable.

Key: ST = Starter, U = Unit

Text

U2: Guardian News and Media Limited for the text from 'How Marvel's superheroes found the magic to make us all true believers' by Jeffrey A Brown, *The Guardian*, 31/08/2013. Copyright Guardian News & Media Ltd 2013.

Photography

The following images are sourced from Getty Images.

UST: Klaus Vedfelt/DigitalVision; Jetta Productions Inc./DigitalVision; Robin Skjoldborg/Cultura; Nikada/E+; monkeybusinessimages/iStock/ Getty Images Plus; andresr/E+; **U1:** Holger Leue/Lonely Planet Images; Leland Bobbe/Stockbyte; Westend61; Eva-Katalin/E+; Daniel Schoenen/ Look; Art Wager/E+; **U2:** Hulton Archive/Moviepix; Pekic/E+; **U3:** guruxoox/iStock/Getty Images Plus; LauriPatterson/E+; Monty Rakusen/ Cultura; Trevor Williams/DigitalVision; Image Source; **U4:** Visions of our Land/Photolibrary; RosLol/Moment; Hill Street Studios LLC/DigitalVision; **U5:** Hero Images; pixelfit/E+; Paul Bradbury/OJO Images; **U6:** vgajic/ E+; Caiaimage/Sam Edwards; Tim Robberts/Taxi; **U7:** Luca Sage/Taxi; Ridofranz/iStock/Getty Images Plus; **U8:** Pierre-Yves Babelon/Moment; Johner Images; Kai-Otto Melau/Getty Images Sport; **U9:** LongHa2006/E+; Colin Hawkins/The Image Bank; Astrakan Images/Cultura; **U10:** Elena Odareeva/iStock Editorial/Getty Images Plus; Ashley Cooper/Corbis NX; SolStock/E+; Tuayai/iStock/Getty Images Plus; Westend61; **U11:** Jon Bower at Apexphotos/Moment Open; View Pictures/Universal Images Group; Eva-Katalin/E+; Westend61; TonTectonix/iStock/Getty Images Plus; **U13:** Manchan/DigitalVision; ranplett/E+; ianmcdonnell/E+; Alfredo Maiquez/ Lonely Planet Images; **U14:** Nick Daly/Cultura; Vladimir Vladimirov/E+; Caiaimage/Chris Ryan/OJO+.

The following images are sourced from other sources/libraries

U2: Serhii Bobyk/Alamy Stock Photo; **U12:** ZUMA Press, Inc./Alamy Stock Photo.

Front cover photography by Supawat Punnanon/EyeEm; Patrick Foto; fStop Images-Caspar Benson.

Illustrations
Chris Chalik

Audio
Produced by Ian Harker and recorded at The SoundHouse Studios, London

Page make up
EMC Design Ltd